It is my privilege to recommend Dimitri Sala's *The Stained Glass Curtain*. He presents with unusual eloquence, firsthand knowledge, and superb scholarship the perspective of a born-again, Spirit-led, Bible-believing Catholic priest who loves his Catholic roots but reaches for the fuller expression of the canopy of the tree of Christianity. God is at work in all branches and expressions of Christianity and Dimitri Sala's book is proof of that.

—Ed Silvoso
Author, *Transformation and Anointed for Business*

So here's this Catholic priest who says he has been born again, that he has accepted Jesus Christ as his personal Lord and Savior, that he uses the Four Spiritual Laws from Campus Crusade for evangelism, that he has enjoyed his work with Promise Keepers, and that he believes individuals who have been baptized as infants need to be evangelized. What is going on here? Answers are found in this compelling book, where Father Dimitri Sala, O.F.M., draws on the Second Vatican Council, the Catholic *Catechism*, statements from the popes, and other Catholic teaching to show how he makes such claims honestly to break down barriers between Catholics and Protestants. While Father Sala is honest about differences between Catholic and Evangelical conceptions of faith, he is convincing that those differences are far less important than what can draw these strands of Christian faith together.

—Mark A. Noll
Francis A. McAnaney Professor of History, Notre Dame
Author, *The Rise of Evangelicalism: The Age of Edwards,
Whitefield, and the Wesleys*
Co-author, *Is the Reformation Over? An Evangelical Assessment
of Contemporary Roman Catholicism*

This book is both informative and challenging. It will challenge you to rethink much of what you have heard concerning Catholic teaching, and inform you of teaching you have not heard that is Catholic. I know Dimitri Sala, and his love for God is evident. He is a saved, Spirit-filled Catholic who believes the truth of the Word and rejects false teaching. Many groups have allowed traditions of men to affect the foundational truths of the faith, including Protestants. We are to contend for the faith once delivered to the saints. We must learn and unlearn things in our pursuit of truth. We must have a Berean spirit, and I believe this is what Dimitri Sala possesses. This will be evident as you read this book. These truths have been followed and preached for generations. They are tried and true, and have been believed and transferred to us from the fathers of the faith. It is time for the present generation to pick up the mantle and carry it and impart it to future generations.

—John Eckhardt
Founder, IMPACT Ministries,
Author, *Prayers that Rout Demons*

I have often wondered if it is possible to remove the divisions between Catholics and Protestants. The theological and cultural barriers seem insurmountable. Yet I believe God has raised up Dimitri Sala for this purpose. He is an Evangelical, Spirit-filled Catholic who feels called by God to this task. He speaks boldly as a prophet to his own Catholic audience, yet he has an important message to Protestants as well. Dimitri is a seasoned theologian and a compassionate priest. But what I love most about him is his passion to see Jesus Christ lifted high as Savior and Lord.

—J. Lee Grady, Contributing Editor, *Charisma Magazine*
Director, The Mordecai Project

Almighty God is using Father Sala to help "heal the divide." This is an urgent message. Perhaps one in a hundred—Evangelical or Catholic— are enjoying the abundant life. Consider this statement, "The quality of a believers' life is in direct proportion to his/her ability to hear and obey the Word of God in the power of the Holy Spirit."

—Bill McCartney
Chairman/CEO, Promise Keepers

As a Native American with more than fifty years of Christian ministry to more than two hundred tribes, I have personally witnessed Christianity continue animosity toward other Christian groups to the point that it has been the focal point of Christian resistance among the tribes of America and Canada. This book by Fr. Dimitri Sala is the good news I have been looking for since my introduction to Christianity. I still believe the Natives are in the "fishbowl" for our turn to have broken walls come down, to see a church united as the Bible so graciously demands. Even today, the division of Christian beliefs has produced the term *White Man's Gospel*, giving the impression that Christianity is too divided, and giving us a reason to resist the good news. This book will take away the hurt and disappointments of Native history concerning the Christian faith in Indian country.

—Dr. Jay Swallow
Minister to Native America

Father Dimitri Sala, my brother in Christ and a Franciscan evangelist, offers clear evidence that official Roman Catholic doctrine and teaching agree with Evangelical teaching that salvation and justification before God are by God's grace and faith in Christ's finished work on the cross. It is time for Catholics and Evangelicals to come together and be led by God's Spirit to obey Jesus' commands to preach the good news of God's Kingdom, to heal the sick, and to pray for revival in this country and in the nations of the world, as the Body of Christ faces the increasing darkness of the End Times. United in Christ we stand—divided we fall.

—GARY S. GREIG, PhD
SENIOR EDITOR, GOSPEL LIGHT PUBLICATIONS

The Stained Glass Curtain is excellent, obviously written from the heart as well as the head. The good news proclaimed by Roman Catholics and Evangelicals should bring us closer together and appreciate the gifts we share. This volume sees the great possibilities that lie in our ongoing ecumenical relationship.

—FR. JAMES LOUGHRAN, SA
DIRECTOR, GRAYMOOR ECUMENICAL & INTERRELIGIOUS INSTITUTE

One of the great impediments to Christian unity is our failure to realize how our vocabularies shape and misshape our understanding of each other. So, when the Protestant tells the Catholic, "Faith alone," the Catholic hears, "Believe and do as you please," and when the Catholic says to the Protestant, "Grace allows us to cooperate with God in our justification," the Protestant hears, "Works righteousness." In both cases, each hears, but does not listen. Father Sala's book is an invitation to really listen, to understand that our traditions, properly understood, may not be as far apart as we think.

—FRANCIS J. BECKWITH
PROFESSOR, PHILOSOPHY, CHURCH-STATE STUDIES, BAYLOR UNIVERSITY
AUTHOR, *RETURN TO ROME: CONFESSIONS OF AN EVANGELICAL CATHOLIC*

My heart rejoiced and tears fell as I read the truth so clearly revealed in *The Stained Glass Curtain*. Father Sala has stripped away all the trappings and gaudy outward garments that have for so long kept the beauty of the gospel hidden. Here, finally, with clarity, the gospel is preached in purity, and it is truly good news. May we prayerfully reflect on the truth in these pages and open our eyes and hearts to the prompting of the Holy Spirit, to His scalpel on our soul, and to the healing and freedom available through the work of Christ on the cross. As for this "fish," I am thrilled to be in the same "fish bowl" and am eternally grateful that the "stained glass curtain" has been lifted.

—PAM STENZEL
DIRECTOR, ENLIGHTEN COMMUNICATIONS

The division among Christian Churches is a scandal and a stumbling block, but it will not be solved either by the vaguely dishonest feel-goodism of the old ecumenism, or by the uncaring acceptance of things as they are. Father Sala's great gifts are that he's honest and that he cares, which make *The Stained Glass Curtain* a serious entry in the ongoing discussion of Christianity.

—JOSEPH BOTTUM
EDITOR, *FIRST THINGS* JOURNAL

This book smashes through the walls of "religion" that divide us and builds a bridge of reconciliation which enables Catholics and Evangelicals to rally around the truth of our shared faith. The gospel message is the power of God unto salvation. Dimitri Sala issues the invitation to lay aside spiritual prejudice and walk in knowledge, love, and unity to effectively build the Body of Christ.

—JANE HAMON
CO-PASTOR, CHRISTIAN INTERNATIONAL FAMILY CHURCH

The Stained Glass Curtain will awaken Protestants and Catholics alike to the power of God's Word. It tears down walls of prejudice and what many believe are doctrinal differences between Protestants and Catholics. Father Sala is an extraordinary minister of the gospel of Christ. He takes the reader to common ground regarding the transformation of the soul and reformation of the person.

—DR. JOHN P. KELLY
CEO, INTERNATIONAL CHRISTIAN WEALTHBUILDERS FOUNDATION
CEO, LEADERSHIP EDUCATION FOR ADVANCEMENT AND DEVELOPMENT

The first time I met Fr. Dimitri, the thought that occurred to me was, "He's a bridge-builder, a trailblazer, and a theologian with an apostolic anointing." *The Stained Glass Curtain* is a brilliant living legacy that will cross-connect us to our common purpose and destiny. It is a must-read for those willing to intelligently break out of the box.

—DR. MICHELLE CORRAL
FOUNDRESS, BREATH OF THE SPIRIT MINISTRIES,
PROPHETIC WORD TELECAST

The Stained Glass Curtain belongs on a required reading list for all who consider themselves Christian. Our world suffers from centuries of ignorance regarding the true core beliefs of Evangelicals and Catholics. Father Sala explores these denominational differences and offers a guide for healing the wounds of division. Those who genuinely seek church unity will find a roadmap in this book.

—BARBARA SHLEMON RYAN, RN
PRESIDENT, BELOVED MINISTRY
AUTHOR, *HEALING PRAYER, TO HEAL AS JESUS HEALED, LIVING EACH DAY BY THE POWER OF FAITH, HEALING THE HIDDEN SELF, AND HEALING THE WOUNDS OF DIVORCE*

This book is about the reconciliation of the Body of Christ and the healing of age-old wounds. Father Dimitri has taken a courageous stand by daring to write a bridge-building book. He deserves to be heard by those who believe God has called His Body to fulfill the Lord's prayer in John 17:21, that we all be one.

—DR. CINDY JACOBS
GENERALS INTERNATIONAL

The story of Dimitri Sala reads like something out of St. Augustine's classic, *Confessions.* But what makes this story unique is the way Fr. Dimitri meticulously shows that Evangelical Protestants and Catholics are one in the saving message of the gospel of Jesus Christ. Multitudes on both sides have yet to see what is demonstrated here. I prayed for a book like this for years. It has the power to launch a "new" reformation/conversion for the whole Church. This is the ecumenism we really need, deeply rooted in the gospel of conversion and new birth.

—DR. JOHN H. ARMSTRONG
PRESIDENT, ACT 3,
AUTHOR, *YOUR CHURCH IS TOO SMALL: WHY UNITY IN CHRIST'S MISSION IS VITAL TO THE FUTURE OF THE CHURCH*

THE STAINED GLASS CURTAIN

FR. DIMITRI SALA, OFM

CREATION
HOUSE
A STRANG COMPANY

THE STAINED GLASS CURTAIN by Fr. Dimitri Sala, O.F.M.
Published by Creation House
A Strang Company
600 Rinehart Road
Lake Mary, Florida 32746
www.strangbookgroup.com

Design Director: Bill Johnson
Cover design: Justin Evans

Library of Congress Control Number: 2010929224
International Standard Book Number: 978-1-61638-181-3
First Edition
10 11 12 13 14—9 8 7 6 5 4 3 2 1
Printed in the United States of America

CONTENTS

ACKNOWLEDGMENTS

T HIS BOOK IS the result of years of spiritual experience and the "vision" birthed therein. But what good is spiritual vision without people who believe in it and embrace it with you?

There are countless individuals and groups with whom I've been blessed to share the contents of this book long before any thought of writing. The joy of seeing their response became a continual motivation to publish. For that I say, "Thanks!"

Among these, may I express special gratitude to the Tent of Meeting, my home-based ministry of fired-up faithful Catholic evangelizers here in Chicago. Also to "The Network," of which the Tent of Meeting is part; those "wild and crazy" individuals and ministries with a passion for evangelism and seeing God's prophetic dreams come to pass in our day. Your consistent encouragement and love have been an untold blessing to me as your spiritual father. I may be the mouthpiece here, but this is "our book."

Thanks to Joanne Olinger for her work on the manuscript, and Amber Backes for her research assistance. Thanks to all my trusted intercessors for praying this project through. Thanks to Allen Quain and the family-like staff of Creation House. You took the risk, and you've been great to work with. I am also grateful to those who spent the time to read and endorse this book. You are giants in what you do. To "Padre Ed," for this book's Foreword which expresses his deeper support for the "vision" of Christian unity.

And for all things (1 Thess. 5:18), thanks to Him-Who-Sits-on-the-Throne. The Ancient of Days. The All-Consuming Fire. My Father, and the Father of all who become His children through the Good News, of which I am not ashamed (Rom. 1:16).

Foreword

FATHER DIMITRI HAS been an integral part of our International Transformation Network. Three things have brought us together: a common faith in the same Jesus as Lord and Savior; a shared burden and vision for seeing the Kingdom of God come to cities and nations around the globe; and in that context, an intentional pursuit for true Bible-based, Spirit-initiated unity in the Body of Christ wherever it is found.

Dimitri Sala is on a journey and so are we. When we first began to pray for cities, God made us the answer to those prayers. We began to work with Evangelical believers in cities to "reach them for Jesus." Prayer, more than preaching, was the key component. Based on Jesus' experience with the seventy in Luke 10, this approach became known as "prayer evangelism"—talking to God about our neighbors before talking to our neighbors about God.

We discovered that by praying that way, the Lord Jesus Himself was brought into the picture to do for the lost what neither we could do for them nor they for themselves. And when He did something as a consequence of such praying, we found ourselves preaching less about our theological differences with Catholics and preaching more about Jesus and what He was doing in the city. As a result, cities began to experience God 24/7, and in the midst of that kind of city movement, we "Evangelicals" began to have some interesting, and even comical at first, breakthrough experiences with our born-again counterparts in the Roman Catholic Church—the ones on the "other side of the street."

In one city, we had initiated a movement of prayer among (Evangelical) Christians to pray for their neighbors. We made up small signs to be placed in the windows of their homes stating, "House of Light: we are praying for our neighborhood here." Not to be "outdone," the Catholics did something similar. In our outreaches, we both were often heard to be singing the same choruses of faith and preaching from the same Bible passages.

At one point, we had determined to visit the entire city with a good news packet (evangelistic tracts and the Gospel of John). Because it was "us" doing it, our counterparts in the Catholic camp thought better of it and counseled their constituents not to receive the packets. But the Lord led us to visit the bishop's house first, before the campaign. We found ourselves learning about our personal experiences with Christ and our common burden to see people saved. The God-inspired interest in doing good for the whole city changed attitudes based on prejudice and eventually redrew the whole picture. Competitiveness and fear gave way to the presence of the Lord Jesus. We ended up praying together that God's "...Kingdom would come and His will would be done, on that city, as it was in heaven," and the bishop instructed his people to receive and read the evangelistic packets.

We have had many similar experiences over the years. In another city, I asked the bishop what vision he had for his ministry. His response surprised and blessed us. He said he wanted to raise up a generation of evangelists who understood the Father's heart and not just His judgment. It was his view that while the Catholic Church's emphasis on punishment of sin was important, it was an incomplete picture of the full gospel. He believed that Evangelicals knew about a relationship with the Father that Catholics had not mastered, and therefore they had something to learn from them.

More recently, I was invited to a Latin American city embroiled in crime, murder, and drugs. It had become evident to civic leaders that such war did not have a chance of being won with soldiers and bullets. Something else was needed. In essence, weapons of a different sort. I invited Father Dimitri to join me because we both knew that only the power of the gospel and the manifest presence of the living Christ could make a difference, and for the city to be saved, that power had to be unleashed through the lives of those who have embraced Him. That week, we ministered together to more than three hundred top business and political influencers, most of them Catholic. We did not talk about theological differences. We did not argue or debate. Together, we presented Jesus, the hope of glory, and it was our joy to see local leaders invite Jesus into their hearts and into the city!

Obviously, God is building His Church and we do not have all the answers. All the details are not resolved yet. But we are both most convinced that Christ is the One doing the building and that His Church will be victorious in discipling the nations.

We are also most aware that today we stand where this book ends—at the beginning. Dimitri Sala's book is a key part of the compass we need in order to continue forward.

Let the journey begin.

—ED SILVOSO
AUTHOR, *ANOINTED FOR BUSINESS AND TRANSFORMATION*,
PRESIDENT AND FOUNDER OF THE INTERNATIONAL
TRANSFORMATION NETWORK

1

The Same Fishbowl

As a Lutheran Christian, my theological understanding and spiritual life were powerfully formed by the formula of "justification by grace alone, through faith alone, because of Christ alone". The truth of the gospel that that formula was intended to protect is, I am convinced, entirely compatible...with the authentic teaching of the Catholic Church.[1]

—RICHARD JOHN NEUHAUS

I am not ashamed to confess that on many points my views have been clarified through my study of the Romish theologians.[2]

—ABRAHAM KUYPER

NOT TOO LONG ago, some scientists conducted an experiment. It began with a water-filled tank divided down the middle by a piece of glass. On one side of the glass the men put a prey-eating pike, on the other, some smaller fish as its food. The larger creature, as to be expected, followed its instinct and swam vigorously toward its meal, only to be hindered by the invisible yet solid wall. As the study continued over the next few days, the pike eventually figured out that the food was unattainable, so it simply stopped itself in its instinctual pursuit. At this point, the barrier was removed. Yet, interestingly enough, the pike's behavior persisted: it no longer headed for the food, even though there was nothing to prohibit it. Hunger instinct or not, the pike functioned as though the barrier, which was no longer present, still existed.[3]

I begin with this true account as a telling parable about a dynamic I've seen active between Catholics and Evangelicals over the last twenty-five years or so. Many people, including me, can tell the story of how we were *caught* on the bait of the gospel of Jesus by "fishers of men." From them we individually heard God's plan of salvation, took whatever time we needed to understand its implications for our particular lives, ultimately fell under its divine conviction about our sin problem, admitted that we were thereby in a desperately, hopelessly, helplessly lost state, repented of that sin problem once and for all, trusted Jesus alone as our Savior, and surrendered to Him as Lord. This, we learned, is the way a person internally accepts God's grace of salvation and enters a new life through Jesus Christ.

So in yielding to God's plan, one can say that we were caught in Christ's net and immersed in the water of baptism. But what happened next was something many of us weren't necessarily planning on, something that caught a lot of us off guard, something that became the greatest challenge yet to face: we were all placed in the *same fishbowl*!

Ah, there's the rub! For, from as far back as the first generation in Corinth, we believers have had quite a time with Jesus' deliberate choice to situate those who were converted *in relationship with one another*. The Corinthians formed groups that couldn't seem to abide with the fact that the Church must function as one indivisible unit. And subsequent Christian history testifies (much to our embarrassment) that later, things *went south* regarding this issue.

Yet God is faithful, and believers have responded to the grace He has poured out in spite of ourselves. The last decades in particular have witnessed a tremendous reawakening among Christian leaders on significant levels. There is an honest pursuit of asking how we are to embrace "swimming in the same fishbowl." In the ranks of ordinary believers, we can observe an increasing desire to reach out across denominational and cultural boundaries. It is evident that something within the members of the Body just can't settle for the way things are between our various groupings. All but the most proud and smug of believers are starting to sense that as God *is* faithful, and we *can* begin to find satisfactory solutions to our unhappy divisions.

Yet, this having been said, we still have a problem. On the one hand the Holy Spirit inspires us to believe that real reconciliation is approachable, on the other, our past experiences seem to declare that there are insurmountable barriers. By faith we affirm what God is capable of doing, even in the realm of Christian unity; but as we follow those *instincts* within—like the pike in the investigation—what we've *learned by experience* keeps us from attaining what is available. As a matter of fact, we've *learned* so well that we *stop short* of what's really accessible.

What is the *experience* to which I refer? For one, in the corporate history of Christianity, critical choices have been made and crucial things spoken, the consequences of which we still live with today. The relationship between Catholics and Evangelicals is a story of power-plays and politics, misunderstandings, and bitterness—all of which have bred a suspicion lasting into our lifetime. Battle lines from past wars—sometimes literal wars—are still drawn, even if only in the realm of ideas and beliefs. And this history is not, nor can it be, magically erased by our good intentions. Like all history, it has become an inherited filter through which one group is *taught* to view the other.

Let me put flesh on these statements as they apply to Catholics and Evangelicals. The Reformation was the historical event from which we can trace our present divisions. The conflict of the Reformation centered on Martin Luther's teaching about how human sinners are made right with a holy God (what the Bible calls "justification"). The Church's leaders at the time had issues with Luther's doctrine, but this was by no means the first doctrinal disagreement in the history of the Church. A standard procedure was initiated for resolution (a procedure which today we might call "listening sessions"). However, midway through the process, the Church hierarchy flexed its ecclesiastical muscles and offered Fr. Martin a premature ultimatum—either recant, or face the consequences. Hence, the conflict was never satisfactorily or even charitably resolved. The unfinished business of the dialogue remained fossilized right where it ended, the open sores continued running, and it was from *there* that the relationship between Evangelical believers and Catholics proceeded. Spiritual or emotional healing was on no one's agenda, so no mature growth through conflict took place. Rather, each side grew increasingly charged up over its position, dug its heels in, and stubbornly resisted the other with calculated assault. The years and centuries ahead added insult to injury as persons, groups, or even whole nations postured against one another over differences, sometimes to the point of bloodshed.

This, then, is the historical flow into which we present-day Evangelicals and Catholics have been inserted. This is the spiritual background which, through no choice of our own, we inherited. These events have been preserved by our respective forebears and related back to us as an explanation of why things are the way they are between us. And as they are related, let's not forget they will naturally be told from the perspective of the teller. Can we then claim that these experiences have not on some level formed our perceptions of one another, Catholic to Evangelical and Evangelical to Catholic? And can we pretend they create no hesitancies toward one another even centuries after their occurrence?

My point is that the historical vein suggesting that Catholic and Protestant differences are irreconcilable runs deep. So deep, I believe, that it still affects our ability to make rational choices about how we view each other even today. Let me hone in on some of the examples of what I mean. Much of our conflictual history polarized us along the lines of right and wrong and falsehood and truth. We got very busy in the pursuit of proving each other sinfully wrong. Because of this, I believe, we still have a hard time seeing each other outside of good guy or bad guy categories. How often today, for instance, would we hear a pastor declaring from the pulpit, "You know, when it comes to (name a subject), we have it wrong; it's they (the *other side*) who have it right"? Or how many of us, if we get deep-down honest, don't still relish a thought that this historical mess would be easily solved if the *other side* would finally just give in and "see it our way"? Or, how often do we operate out of the stereotypes history has taught us—let's say that gut-level skepticism which infers, "no matter what they *say*, Catholics still think they're saved by works," or, "Evangelicals just want an easy way to heaven bought by cheap grace"? What about that pre-conscious distrust which surmises that an Evangelical doesn't have an obedient bone in his body or which suspects the Catholic Church's hidden agenda is to bring us all back to Rome?

Let's just name this for what it is: outside the sphere of religion, the inherited historical filter we've been talking about is called prejudice—from the Latin *prae* and *judicium*, to "judge beforehand." Yes, both Catholics and Evangelicals have sustained some of the pre-conceived judgments which history has played out between our two groups. The point is this: insofar as the prejudices we've *learned* from the experiences of history persist in our relationships, we can be sure we will not attain the unity that the Spirit prompts in our hearts.

There's another source of experience besides the past—the present. If I operate with prejudice to begin with, it's not hard to find present evidence persuading me that my skewed judgments are true. Someone once said, "If you go out looking for a bear, you'll find it." It is of the nature of prejudice to self-fulfill; because it governs our perceptions, we will end up seeing exactly what we want to see. We will also much more easily generalize on individual experiences and steer away from other evidence which may outdate or challenge our judgments. Thus, our prejudices will be reinforced as we *learn* by our experiences.

Again, let me concretize. Does the Catholic Church teach its adherents to worship statues? Is it a tenet of Evangelicalism to disrespect Catholics? Is it true that there are no saved people in the Catholic Church? Do Evangelicals believe that real Christianity basically stopped after the apostles, and only picked up again with Martin Luther? These questions articulate pre-judgments Catholics and Evangelicals have toward one another—judgments for which either group might find what it considers to be ample supporting evidence today. For there *are* Catholics who have idolatrous relationships with religious art,

Evangelicals who *do* "Catholic-bash," people in the Catholic Church who are *not* in a saving relationship with Jesus Christ, and Evangelicals who *are* ignorant of the fifteen centuries of Catholic history between biblical times and the Reformation. But a non-prejudiced heart will carefully weigh in the fact that his or her experience with such people is qualified: it is subjective, and it is limited. To the extent we draw conclusions through the lenses of present prejudice fashioned by the conditioning of history, we will surely not attain the unity our spiritual instincts prompt in our hearts.

Be assured, there is a plethora of stories we all could tell about pre-judgments running the opposite denominational direction. The point is this: the invisible spiritual wall stopping us from attaining the unity for which Jesus so fervently prayed is not what we might be quick to conclude it is. Factors such as historical hurts, inherited pain, political alienation, and even doctrinal disputes are important to recognize; but let us not forget that these are issues with which the Church has always had to struggle. We have had success, however, only when we approached such conflicts with an attribute called *openness.* Many Catholic-Evangelical conflicts remain conflicts today because of a deeper issue: we have failed on some level to come to each other in a trusting openness. We have, rather, operated with a fear that listening openly to each other's positions will somehow destroy what we, ourselves, hold dearest as believers. Trusting one another and God as He works in the process is difficult and leaves us vulnerable. It means we may have to admit the error of our "filters" and learn *from* one another instead of *about* one another. Far easier it is to run for cover in our prejudices. But it is these prejudices that the Enemy uses as the invisible barrier which stops the Lord from what He is capable of doing to unite us. And as a result, though in a post-Iron Curtain era, Christians have maintained their own "Stained Glass Curtain" of suspicion and mistrust.

GOOD NEWS

But there is also some good news about this dilemma. The scriptures tell us that where there is fear, God's love has not found its complete home in us (cf. 1 John 4:18). Yet the same verse also says that where His perfect love is present, fear is cast out. In other words, if we can but acknowledge the fear of what we'll lose by being vulnerably open to one another, and the fear causing us to lock each other up in prejudice, but then open up to the *Lord* with that fear, His perfect love will deal with it. Unity is of the Spirit (cf. Eph. 4:3), and if we really want it, we will be *given* that trust and love by our Paraclete. He *wants* to provide what we need in order to follow the instincts toward unity which He Himself generated in our hearts.

And the other point of good news is that He *has* provided. In one part of our "fishbowl" that invisible barrier has already been removed. Yes, in one specific area, the reason for us to maintain judgments against each other has already been taken out. The problem is that—like the pike in the experiment—we're still acting as if it's still in place. What is the area to which I am referring? It's the most important of them all, the very foundation of the Church, the basis upon which all else in Christianity is built: the gospel. Yes, in this book I hope to demonstrate that on the level of evangelizing with the message of salvation and because of the working of the Holy Spirit, official Catholic teaching and the preaching of Evangelicals *do not differ*.

It is interesting that in the intense theologizing which has accompanied Christian ecumenism lately, there's a "still, small voice" which it seems only a few are picking up. Perhaps because I am an evangelist involved in apostolic ministry, it's been easier to identify it. But it is a call for the cause of Christian unity to return to its foundation, the gospel. Listen as Paul Molnar, a Catholic, speaks of (the now late Cardinal) Avery Dulles' assessment of the finalized *Joint Declaration on the Doctrine of Justification* signed by the Lutheran World Federation and the Catholic Church in 1999:

> And he [Avery Dulles] concludes by noting that it is not enough to say Lutherans and Catholics use different frameworks for thinking about justification; rather it must be shown that Lutheran and Catholic thinking derive from the same gospel.[4]

Geoffrey Wainwright, a non-Catholic responding to John Paul II's document *That They May Be One* states:

> ...the Pope should invite those Christian communities which he regards as being in real, if imperfect, communion with the Roman Catholic Church to appoint representatives to cooperate with him and his appointees in formulating a statement expressive of the Gospel to be preached to the world today. Thus the theme of "fraternal dialogue" which John Paul II envisaged would shift...to the *substance* of what is believed and preached.[5]

Though not written specifically as a response to these theologians, the book you are reading nevertheless answers their call. Its goal is to show that, when it comes to the gospel, "the substance of what is believed and preached" in evangelicalism and in official Catholic teaching is part of what the Second Vatican Council of the Catholic Church called "our common heritage."[6]*

A Book for Us

This book is written for both Evangelicals and Catholics. For Evangelicals because among these brethren it is not unheard of to claim that the Catholic Church preaches a different, and therefore false, gospel. Many Evangelicals do withhold such an assertion; but understandably they may still find themselves unsure of how the gospel and the Catholic Church fit together. These fellow believers would be gratified to know, I hope, that I was confronted with these very issues soon after my conversion and that this put me on a diligent personal search for answers. But, while I could not deny a false works-based gospel was indeed widely preached by Catholic leaders, I also discovered that those leaders were out of harmony with the official teachings of my Church. The Second Vatican Council had even expressed its concern over this very tendency among the Catholic Church's most visible leaders—its priests:

> ...the task of priests is not to teach their own wisdom, but God's Word, and to summon all

---

* I am not unaware of the very fine work of Evangelicals and Catholics Together, (ECT) an interdenominational group of theologians and Christian leaders that, in its 1997 statement entitled, "The Gift of Salvation," articulated points of our unity on this topic (www.seekgod.ca/ect2.htm). The book you are reading differs from that briefer statement in three ways: 1) I am limiting my focus to the *content* of the message that brings salvation; 2) I document official Catholic teaching which supports the propositions of the message; and most importantly, 3) in the description of the message's content, I pick up at a point where ECT stops short—it doesn't specify what constitutes the *kind* of faith that saves. The belief about exactly *how* a person is saved through faith still poses a perceived barrier between Catholics and Evangelicals. I will demonstrate through official Catholic teaching that, even here, we have a "common heritage."

men urgently to conversion and holiness (*Decree on the Ministry and Life of Priests*, 4).[7]

By contrast, when I researched what my Church really does teach on salvation, I was delighted to find that *the gospel was there*!

One of the goals of this publication, then, is to "set the record straight" by providing Evangelical readers with accurate information, taken directly from Catholic primary sources. As a matter of fact, I intend to employ a format popularly used by many Evangelicals—the Four Spiritual Laws[8]—and confirm that each truth therein is also supported by Catholic documentation. In doing so, my hope is to expose the lies the Enemy uses to build the barrier of suspicion between Evangelicals and Catholics and to say to my born-again brethren, "That part of the invisible wall is gone!" I am happy to report that believers who have heard this material at live teachings have responded with enthusiasm, and I haven't ceased praising God for the tangible steps to unity paved at these events. I pray the same will happen as a result of these written pages.

This book is also addressed to Catholics. There are many of us, first of all, who fit the description at the beginning of this chapter: we have already heard, understood, and personally responded to God's plan of salvation, and by this conversion, regard ourselves "born again" no less than our Evangelical brethren. But for us, there is a predicament: we face suspicion by some of our members that we are not really Catholic (and sometimes even become the object of their persecution), while on the other hand, some of our brother Evangelicals doubt our salvation simply because we chose to remain in our Church. It's the pain of being "neither fish nor fowl." This text, then, is also written to equip such Catholics who have entered a saving relationship with Jesus, that we need no longer apologize for being both born again and Catholic nor shrink back from sharing this same gospel with others—including those in our own Church. This book will illustrate just how *Catholic* the Four Spiritual Laws are.

And that leads to another type of Catholic for whom this book is designed. There are those in my Church who have heard the message of salvation either in whole or in part, but have dismissed it because it "sounds too Protestant" (a common Catholic prejudgment). There are also those who have heard and not dismissed the message, but have legitimate questions about how their Catholic identity harmonizes with the gospel. For these types of Catholics this book will demonstrate that, whether coming from a Protestant or Catholic source, the gospel is still part of the common heritage of Christianity we share with all who preach it.

I can't tell you how many perceptions have been changed—Catholic about Evangelical and Evangelical about Catholic—by this information. Yes, Satan has succeeded in keeping us ignorant of important information about each other. Indeed, one of *Webster's* definitions of the word *prejudice* is "an opinion or leaning adverse to anything without just grounds or *before sufficient knowledge*" (emphasis added). I hope this knowledge will substantiate the good news that at least one reason for the invisible barrier between us has been removed: the need to stay apart because of different gospels. That need no longer exists. The Enemy has been quite content to keep this fact hidden from us. If he can but perpetuate his lies, he can keep us, like that pike, uninterrupted in our learned behavior of the past. It's time to publicize the information, disclose the knowledge, and expose the lies that still serve to keep us from unity.

At the very first Promise Keepers event I attended, the session leader quoted something from PK founder, Bill McCartney. It made a deep impression upon me that I haven't forgotten more than a decade later. Coach McCartney said there are two giants left undefeated in the Body of Christ: racism and denominationalism. He explained that, like the giant Goliath did in the Old Testament, these two mock the people of God today: they mock our desire to live the New Testament unity to which we are called (cf. Col. 3:15), and they mock our ability to demonstrate that Jesus Christ is, indeed, the Savior sent by God (cf. John 17:21).[9] This book is my attempt to confront that giant of denominational division. I don't pretend it's the only such undertaking in the Body of Christ today, but I do share the same Spirit-led inspiration motivating my brothers and sisters: It's time to take that giant out!

WOUNDED SOLDIER

Such bold declaration, however, does not come without its price—this book is also written out of pain. If you've been around the Kingdom long enough, you know that pain is what God seems to use to get our attention about the deeper things He wants done. In particular, reconcilers are broken people: firsthand experience is what sensitizes them to the issues of disunity; I am one who has been *sensitized*. For example, I am one of those Catholics described earlier who have felt alienation by some Evangelicals. Among other behaviors, some of the brethren who were suspicious that I wasn't really born again have aggressively quizzed me, only to conclude, "Well, he may be Catholic...but he's saved, alright." Likewise, some in my Church who have not heard the gospel—and some who have—question whether I'm really Catholic, or even ordained.

"And you *are* a Catholic priest, right?" Yes, I, too, know what it's like to be "neither fish nor fowl." I've also listened for years to stories of Catholics who receive the gospel from our ministry or from sources outside their usual church encounters, but who then become rightfully angry that the message had not been presented in their Catholic experience or angry that their Church was then incapable of discipling them once they were converted. And then there are the hours upon hours of ministering to people within or without who have simply been hurt by leaders and/or members of the Catholic Church.

After enough of these painful experiences, I began to feel in my very bowels a kind of grief—grief because lack of relational openness and dialogue has left us all in such a state. And the grief did not cover only personal effects, such as I've described, it was also about the fact that our disunity *radically lessens what God is able to do through us to transform the world by our witness of the gospel.* All this is the pain of Paul who, when confronting the identical issue in Corinth, responded with the anguished question, "Is Christ divided?" (1 Cor. 1:13, NAB). It is the pain of observing the same Christian phenomenon escalate over the centuries and finally manifest in the bitter rivalry of the Reformation era. It is the pain which my Church leadership has voiced in modern times, from the Second Vatican Council's *Decree on Ecumenism* in 1964 expressing "remorse over [our] divisions,"[10] to various subsequent statements,* all summarized (in my opinion) by John Paul II's declaration that

---

* John Paul II has undoubtedly given the clearest voice to this pain during his papacy. For example: 1) "sad years of division" (address, Canterbury Cathedral, May 29, 1982), 5; 2) "sad history of past enmities" (address, Leaders of Christian Churches, Murrayfield, England, June 1, 1982), 3; 3) "hurt from the controversies of the past" (address, Cardinals and Curia, June 28, 1985), 9; 4) "[the Church's] painful past and hurt which regrettably continues to provoke even today," "deplorable division," and "painful human reality of [the Church's] divisions" (*That They May Be One*, Rome, May 25, 1995), 2, 22.

"ecclesial communion has been painfully wounded" and Christian schisms constitute a "painful chapter of history."[11]

Once again, let me emphasize that there *have* been strides emanating from various levels of Christian life, toward reconciliation. At the grass roots, Evangelicals and Catholics have prayed and fellowshiped side-by-side increasingly over the last decades, especially at events sponsored by the charismatic renewal. Likewise, we have linked up on social or political issues too important to stay apart about; starting in 1985, some theologians and ministerial leaders issued the "Evangelicals and Catholics Together" statements, which not only expressed hope and commitment toward full unity, but also articulated and affirmed the sure bases upon which unity already exists. These statements also opened a door for intelligent critique and debate on the positions taken therein.

On the level of official Church leadership, advances have been gained as well. The Catholic Church has taken responsibility for its part in the disastrous events of the Reformation,* confessed its sins of disunity,[12] and more than once sought forgiveness from those whom we have offended in this way.[13] Eager to speed the process of reconciliation, John Paul II issued a watershed message in 1995, *That They May Be One*, which not only articulated the Catholic Church's seriousness about pursuing full unity at this hour but also suggested principles by which this may be achieved ([healthy] "fraternal dialogue"[14]). The *Joint Declaration on the Doctrine of Justification* and accompanying statements of clarification were mutually endorsed by the Vatican and by the Lutheran World Federation on Reformation Day, October 31, 1999. Though not without its critics, this official statement of

---

* "But in subsequent centuries more widespread disagreements appeared and quite large Communities became separated from full communion with the Catholic Church—developments for which, at times, men of both sides were to blame," Vatican II, *Decree on Ecumenism*, 3.

both communions put a major dent in reconciling the pivotal *hot potato* of the Reformation—the doctrinal differences in understanding the phrase "justification by faith."

However, in none of these statements—official or unofficial— do we find a watering-down of the differences that still remain between the groups.* Each collection of Christians maintains the integrity of its own convictions and acknowledges that true unity will not result from mere diplomacy or compromise. Rather, the spirit that prevails can be described by a phrase from the *Joint Declaration* where its signers were said to be "in their difference open to one another."[15]

Yes, progress has been made—unprecedented, as a matter of fact, given the preceding centuries of Reformation and Counter Reformation Church history. Yet the fact remains that much lies yet unreconciled and in broken pieces. As a member of the Body, I certainly rejoice in the healing that has taken place. The Scripture says that when one part of a body is glorified, the other parts share it (cf. 1 Cor. 12:26). Yet, the same verse assures us that when one part agonizes, the others do likewise (the Greek word used is *sym-paschein*, to suffer or feel pain together). It is this pain yet remaining in the Body, and in me as part of the Body, along with the sincere desire to see us healed, which has put a charge on me to write this book.

So, may we begin? And as we do, I want to thank God for and celebrate whatever led you to pick up this book in the first place and to affirm the openness it took to read thus far. Also,

---

* Before his election to the papacy, Benedict XVI occupied the role of Prefect of the Doctrine of the Faith, whose ratification the *Joint Declaration on the Doctrine of Justification* would have had to have gained before being signed by the Catholic Church. Richard John Neuhaus states that the then-Cardinal Ratzinger had "written witheringly about an old liberal style of ecumenism that tried to overcome division by 'negotiating' differences, as though the Christian reality was a matter of diplomacy and not of divinely revealed truth," (Neuhaus, "The Catholic Difference," *Evangelicals and Catholics*, 215.) Likewise, the signers of the ECT Statement declare, "We reject any appearance of harmony that is purchased at the price of truth," (ECT Statement, xvii).

as a Catholic priest, I'd like to challenge my fellow Church members to continue reading with an open mind and an open heart. I pray that you will hear the voice of the Lord speaking not only through His Word but also through His Body, the Church. And, my Evangelical friends, let me encourage you to stay open as well. This book will no doubt probe some of your beliefs about Catholicism and surface them for re-examination. As for the temptation to draw any hard or fast conclusions, may I invoke the age-old challenge issued by Native Americans—walk the proverbial mile in my moccasins. That walk, I am convinced, will afford sure steps to reconciliation and unity in the Body of Christ.

May we pray?

> *Lord,*
> > *You're summoning us to newer levels*
> > *Than we've ever experienced before,*
> > *As uncomfortable as that may be for us.*
> > *So I align myself with Your desire in Eph. 4:3*
> > *That we do all we can*
> > *To preserve the spirit of unity*
> > *In the bond of peace.*
> > *Teach me,*
> > *Show us all,*
> > *How unnecessary our defensiveness is;*
> > *For no matter what "constructions" we make in the*
> *Body,*
> > *You work on both sides of the wall.*

2

THE SOURCES

I N THE '90s, I was honored by an invitation to member-
ship on the Steering Committee of our Chicago regional
Promise Keepers office. It was a time of rich experiences,
not the least of which was the beginning of a friendship that
has lasted until today with a staff person named Pastor Anthony Earl. The relationship was and still is a mutual lesson in
"Christian covenant despite diversity." He's African-American,
I'm European-American; he's not affiliated with a denomination, I'm Catholic; and the list of our differences goes on and
on, down to our personality styles.

What initially marked his relational seriousness, however,
was that at one of our meetings after I had been attending
regularly, Anthony publicly esteemed the fact that a portion
of the Catholic Church was represented on the Committee.
Trusting then, I presume, in his knowledge that I was indeed
a saved brother in Christ, Anthony asked me to prepare a presentation for the Committee on how a person can be born
again and Catholic at the same time. *Help us understand*, was
his exact request.

I could not doubt Anthony's sincerity. And, looking back
now, I can see he was demonstrating one of PK's biblical principles of reconciliation and Goliath slaying:

> Sensitivity: we must seek knowledge about our
> brothers in order to relate empathetically to
> people from different denominations, tradi-
> tions, races, social standings, or cultures.[1]

This is the principle by which we learn to walk in each other's moccasins, thus building bridges instead of walls.

The first step for one who is open to "walking in my moccasins" is to understand exactly what is meant by a term already
used: official Catholic teaching. And in this step Catholics and
Protestants alike will face the first challenge. The first chapter
already highlighted the role experience plays in our impressions
of one another. In order to move forward, we need to suspend
those impressions momentarily, because "official Catholic
teaching" will seem radically out of sync with what many have
learned by experience to associate with the term *Catholic*.

Here's a "for instance" that has to do just with Church
practices. Did you know that there are married priests in the
Catholic Church? Catholics and Protestants alike may be unaware of the fact that the Catholic Church is comprised of
two segments—the Latin (or Western) Church, and the Ori-
ental (or Eastern) Church. And, though both are under the
Pope, many jurisdictions of the Eastern Church legitimately
continue the more ancient tradition of married priests, never
having decided to restrict priestly ordination to celibates as the
Latin Church later did. So, not only *are* there married Catholic
priests today, but there has never been a time in the Church
when there *weren't* married men in this office. However, many
in the West who base their beliefs on their experience alone and
who have never had exposure to Eastern Catholicism (which
exists in Western countries as well), erroneously conclude that
our Church doesn't allow priests to marry. Some, thereby, even

surmise that we think the nature of the priesthood demands celibacy when, in fact, our teaching says the exact opposite.[2] In this case, then, inaccurate impressions are formed because our experience has not provided enough information, and we simply remain in a state of ignorance. Even in this issue of our ecumenical relations, we arrive at the truth only after we are capable of suspending conclusions based on experience alone.

Suspending what experience has taught us is something we easily do in some other contexts (for example, when we read science fiction, or view a fantasy-based film such as *The Lord of the Rings*). At other times it is simply demanded of us. If you've lived or worked among people (even in our own society) from backgrounds other than your own, you quickly find that the ability to *adapt* has all to do with letting go of some dear assumptions by which you've lived life and then acknowledging some new ones. As a matter of fact, ordinary lived life requires this once in awhile. The Promise Keepers study book on biblical reconciliation gives an example: you encounter a man in a store whose kids are obviously out of control and in their horseplay one of them runs into you and nearly knocks you down. You are obviously irritated and have already drawn some conclusions about this dad and his ability to keep his kids in line. But then the man comes up and apologizes, explaining that his wife died suddenly, that he is still in a daze about it all, and because the kids don't really understand why their mother isn't around, they're behaving in a more hyperactive way than usual. At that point, because of *information*, you receive a *revelation* that causes a change of perception and response.[3]

Rarely, however, do we do the same with our observations across the Catholic–Evangelical divide. Information can not only inform our ignorance, it can also provide revelation—but only if we are willing to suspend our judgments long enough to receive it. Thus I am prompted to ask for a temporary *hold* on your experience-based denominational perceptions and assumptions, no matter how cherished they are and no matter how true they seem. Please allow the official Catholic sources to speak on their own terms, even if they contradict what you've concluded about Catholics and Catholicism by experience. Even Catholics have found it a challenge to approach their faith *document-based* rather than by what their religious experience of the past has *told* them.

This will lead to yet another potential challenge. Follow the logic here:

1. Thinking Christians of all denominations agree that the scriptures should not be used out of context. Proof texting (quoting verses of the Bible simply to back up one's belief, irrespective of how these verses relate with the rest of the Bible) can be dangerous. History contains more than its share of Christians *justifying* things like racism or anti-Semitism by quoting the Bible. Proper use of this primary source of Christian life requires a willingness to take into consideration what we call "the whole counsel of Scripture."

2. It is the nature of religious faith that one cannot have it in theory. Just as one cannot really know what swimming is like without swimming or what driving a car is like without getting behind the wheel and driving, one cannot know what faith is about until he or she actually *believes*. As both St. Augustine and St. Anselm claim in their theology,

understanding the faith is impossible outside of actually *having* faith: one only understands as a participant. Comprehension is ultimately inaccessible to an "outside observer" of faith.*

3. Therefore, specific expressions of the Christian faith cannot be fully known except from within, either. Only a Protestant can ultimately know what it's like to be Protestant, only an Orthodox can know what it's like to ascribe to Orthodoxy, and only a Catholic can articulate the fullness of what it means to be Catholic. The "faith that was once for all handed down to the holy ones [saints]", (Jude 3, NAB), is greater than doctrinal propositions alone. Doctrine is certainly the fundamental ingredient, but faith also includes the lived Christian life and the worship that our doctrine engenders.** So, each specific expression of faith is uniquely known only by those who actually live it.

4. By putting these premises together we can draw some conclusions about the challenge of understanding Catholicism properly. First, those from outside this expression of faith can be prone to evaluate our doctrine and life inaccurately simply by being an outside observer. Second, this can easily occur even in a study of official Catholic

---

* "Unless you believe, you shall not understand." St. Augustine, *Sermons* 18.3, and *Epistles* 70.1.3–4; St. Anselm, *Proslogium* 1.

** Thus we can say, "Now what was handed on by the apostles includes everything which contributes to the holiness of life, and the increase in faith of the People of God; and so the Church, in her teaching, life and worship, perpetuates and hands on to all generations all that she herself is, and all that she believes," (Vatican II: *Dogmatic Constitution on Divine Revelation*, 8.)

documents if statements are taken out of the context of the whole of Catholic teaching. Catholics and Protestants alike have been guilty of proof texting each other's pronouncements without attempts to take seriously the full line of teaching and lived faith which produced those pronouncements. The continual challenge when studying Catholic Church documents, then, is to resist the "Ah-hah! See! I told you!" response. The challenge, as stated by the *Joint Declaration*, is to stand "in [our] difference, open to one another."[4] The call is to revolt against the factious spirit decried in 1 Corinthians and enter into "fraternal dialogue."[5]

My goal, then, is to introduce the reader to what might be called "the whole counsel of teaching" in the Catholic Church. Catholicism can only be evaluated equitably by those who are willing to take into account how its distinct parts are nuanced by the full compilation of its teaching.

CATHOLIC SOURCES

What exactly are these *documents*, and what makes them so significant to Catholicism?

First of all, every denomination has official statements regarding doctrines that the group holds to be true. Some of them come from the corridors of Christian history, such as the Nicene Creed, written in the fourth century but still ascribed to by all Christians.* Other statements represent the beliefs of a particular

---

* The historical Christian Church has used the statements from these early councils to define what correct (orthodox) Christian belief is and what is, indeed, heresy. There are, however, groups which ascribe to heretical beliefs yet still call themselves Christians. The Mormons and the United Pentecostals, for example, do not adhere to the doctrine of the Trinity.

communion, such as the seventeenth century Westminster Confession of Faith governing the beliefs of Presbyterians. Still others express the position of a group of denominations that share doctrinal commonality, such as the more recent 1978 Chicago Statement on Biblical Inerrancy produced by a cross-denominational conference of Evangelicals. There are even phrases which articulate doctrines that can be traced back to the beginning of one particular Christian movement: the term *sola Scriptura*, for example, is a byword of the Protestant teaching that Scripture, and it alone, carries the ultimate authority in Christian life. Likewise, it is a common phenomenon nowadays to see a Statement of Faith written by a particular church congregation, independent ministry, or parachurch organization on its Web site or in its publicity.

So, Christian groups can read the same sourcebook (the Bible), yet still find the need to articulate what they regard as the proper way to understand what it reveals. Sometimes that need arises in response to controversy, when a group must verbalize a particular position believed to be true as distinct from opposing beliefs of others calling themselves Christians. Some classic examples would be the difference among born-again Christians on whether the gifts of the Spirit are still for today, or whether a person's salvation, once properly accepted, is eternally secure.

The Catholic Church is no different in its need to articulate such teaching. At various times our leadership has drafted statements that represent the position of our Church on various topics. But it is important to distinguish between official and unofficial Catholic teaching. Any Catholic can teach or publish on any aspect of our Church life or doctrine, but that does not make him or her an authority with the capacity to speak *of-*

ficially for our Church. Official, or primary, sources are ones written or spoken by those who have the *office* to represent the Catholic Church. Secondary, or unofficial, teaching is that which comments on primary or official sources. The reason this delineation is so important is that a vast segment of Catholics and Evangelicals alike have based their beliefs about Catholicism on *secondary* sources, without realizing that these may or may not accurately portray the official stance of the Catholic Church. What are these primary sources, then?

First, we have the writings of official Christian teachers in the centuries following New Testament times—the Church fathers. They give us a portrait of how Christian life perdured, show us how the Church responded to various issues and conflicts, and forged some of the great doctrines which define what the historical Church believes about Jesus. Included in this group are men like Irenaeus of Lyons, who refuted the first major heresy in Christian history (Gnosticism); Athanasius of Alexandria, a prime architect of the doctrine of the Trinity; and Augustine of Hippo, whose teaching formed much of Western Christianity's thinking on grace and sin, eventually including the thinking of Martin Luther and the Reformation.

As do non-Catholics, we also esteem the teaching of other heroes in Christian history. For Catholics this category would include the writings of some of the saints who lived outside the classical era of the fathers (understood in their proper historical contexts), particularly those whose insights have been affirmed by their contemporaries and by subsequent generations.

In addition, there is the very direct primary source of official Catholic statements. These include:

Documents produced by Church councils

For example, the Nicene Creed derives its name from the fact that it was the pronouncement of the bishops at the Council of Nicaea. The most important council documents for today are those produced by the Second Vatican Council, which took place from 1962–1965. The very purpose of this council was to bring our Church more effectively up to date with current times, so its documents have continued to chart the course of the Catholic Church even to the present.

Official teachings and statements of the popes and the Magisterium

It is important to understand here that there are various levels of papal pronouncements. His personal opinions, though spoken in addresses or messages, obviously do not weigh as heavily as his officially articulated teachings. And, for the sake of clarity, the Pope's statements are not infallible unless he specifically declares the intention to enunciate an infallible teaching—something that has happened only rarely in history. The Magisterium is the official teaching arm of the Catholic Church, which issues statements on various topics. Examples of magisterial teaching would be the Declaration by the Vatican Congregation for the Doctrine of the Faith entitled, *On the Unicity and Salvific Universality of Jesus Christ and the Church* or the *Joint Declaration on the Doctrine of Justification* signed by the Catholic Church and the Lutheran World Federation.

The *Catechism of the Catholic Church*

Promulgated in 1992, this was an attempt to compile, in a contemporary way, teachings on the basic areas of Christian Catholic life. A worldwide consultation of bishops and theologians contributed to its content.

Official statements by bishops

This includes declarations by individual or groups of bishops addressing specific issues within their regions. As stated about the Pope, bishops' personal opinions or other such statements do not carry the same weight as their official teachings about a subject.

Instructions

These are explanatory teachings which preface each liturgical ritual book. They give proper understanding of the sacraments and of other forms of corporate prayer in the Catholic Church.

Secondary sources include any writings of theologians, leaders, or the like, who do not have the office of speaking officially for Catholicism. These sources also include statements by those who *do* have that office when they speak other than for the purpose of an official teaching. The significance of all these sources, of course, depends on the position in the Catholic Church of the person speaking or writing.

Our exploration will take us mostly into primary sources; reputable secondary sources will be cited to round off the primary ones. One final but important note on the use of sources: later ones can clarify, or even correct, earlier ones. The Vatican Council declared:

> Therefore, if the influence of events or of the times has led to deficiencies in conduct, in Church discipline, or even in the formation of doctrine (which must be carefully distinguished from the deposit itself of faith), these should be appropriately rectified in the proper moment (*Ecumenism*, 6).[6]

This statement embodies Luther's concept, *ecclesia semper reformanda,* (the Church must always be reformed). There is an essential unchanging deposit of faith, but the way the Church has attempted to express it from generation to generation is subject to evaluation and, if necessary, to change.

The reason this is so important is that a way of using sources out of context is to insist on a view of Catholicism based on outdated teachings, even though they have been *rectified* by newer ones. To maintain, for example, that the Catholic Church officially promulgates the hatred of Jews found in anti-Semitic writings of some of the Church fathers (or for that matter, so do Protestants, based on statements of Luther) is to deny that correction has been made. In any relationship where there has been injury and alienation, both parties can refuse the other the grace of reform. Though this is normal when one is in pain, relational repairs can only happen when the hurt parties give each other a chance to reevaluate and reposition. The same is true between groups. Biblical reconciliation starts with extending the grace that allows the other to change. This text, then, challenges the reader to reformulate his or her perception and base it on the up-to-date, rectified sources cited.

Let's proceed, then, into an exploration of the role and content of the message of salvation in *official* Catholic sources.

3

THE FIRST PROCLAMATION

MOSTLY EVERYONE HAS heard of the Leaning Tower of Pisa. Its famous flaw began to appear in 1178, even before the tower's completion, and ever since, people have been trying to figure out why it leaned and what could be done about it. All kinds of theories emerged on the first question, including the idea that the original builder designed it so. By the twentieth century, however, the prevailing opinion of architectural engineers who studied the phenomenon was that the tower was simply built on ground unstable for such a tall and heavy structure. The city of Pisa rises only six feet above sea level and is situated on a riverbed, so its underlying ground is composed of uneven layers of sand and clay. The scientists concluded, thereby, that the weight of the building simply compressed the ground on the side that leans.

There have been, of course, various attempts to correct the problem. After being abandoned in 1185 by its first architect with only three and one half floors finished, a second builder ninety years later thought he'd solve the issue by adding another three and one half tiers designed to balance the slant. It didn't work. Eighty years later, a third architect erected the domed eighth floor on the top for the same purpose. Still the tower leaned.

Twentieth century engineers took a crack at it with their sophisticated technology. In 1934, an attempt was made to drill holes into the base of the leaning side and fill them with mortar. The result? The holes further weakened the density of the ground, making the tower lean even more. In 1993, hundreds of tons of lead were hung from the top of the taller side. This seemed to forestall the leaning process but did not ultimately prevent it. Two years later, scientists even tried freezing the ground under the weaker side with liquid nitrogen, then, in a somewhat surgical fashion, they replaced stones in that ground with metal rods for greater support. Paradoxically, this brought the tower the nearest to collapse that it had ever come.

Finally, in 1999, experts began a careful two-year process by which they simply removed ground from under the site gradually. This work stabilized the tower back to its position in 1838, making it predictably safe again, at least for a time. The fact remains, however, that no permanent correction has been found.[1]

This somewhat curious history leads to a simple conclusion: The Leaning Tower of Pisa is a structure that needs nothing less than a foundation makeover. All attempts at straightening the lean while the tower still stood on a questionable foundation and all architectural band-aids or cosmetic surgeries employed could not correct the problem. As a matter of fact, some contributed to the problem, even at the risk of jeopardizing the very existence of the tower itself. History seems to show that the lean could only have been rectified if, when it was discovered, the building was disassembled and erected again on a proper foundation. Even today, scientists say the only guarantee that the tower will stop leaning is a rebuilt base. In the end, common sense won the day: there's simply no substitute for the appropriate foundation.

The exact same is true about the spiritual edifice we call the Catholic Church. Over time, its structure has begun a slow lean back to the earth—power-politicking, corruption, immorality, clericalism, wars, persecutions, racism, etc. Various reforms or correctives have been attempted. Some have effected cosmetic improvements; others have only made the situation worse in the long run.

But in recent times, an insight has dawned on the leadership of my Church: what we have here is a *foundational* issue. Our teaching has acknowledged, for example, that there are those who "have a certain faith, but an imperfect knowledge of the foundations of that faith" (*On Evangelization in the Modern World*, 11).[2] Even in Catholic beliefs, it must be regarded that some truths are, of their very nature, based on more important ones:

> ...in Catholic teaching there exists an order or "hierarchy" of truths, since they vary in their relationship to the foundation of the Christian faith.[3]
>
> —VATICAN II (*ECUMENISM*, 11)

> In the message which the Church proclaims there are certainly many secondary elements. Their presentation depends greatly on changing circumstances. They themselves also change. But there is an essential content, the living substance, which cannot be modified or ignored...[4]
>
> —POPE PAUL VI (*ON EVANGELIZATION*, 25)

Texts such as these point our Church back in the direction of appreciating the importance of what underscores everything in the "household of faith."

My guess is that this very idea may surprise or confuse some of my Catholic readers for many were taught that every element of Catholicism is of equal value. But consider this example again—people have asked why the Leaning Tower of Pisa isn't simply moved to another foundation. In response, it has been said that some Pisans would rather that the tower fall than that it be completely straightened. Why? I would guess this: its serious defect has now been transformed into a drawing card for the city! The tower "as is" has put a relatively small burg on the map, as well as considerably increased its revenue through tourism. In that process, however, it cannot be denied that the tower now serves a whole new purpose. Its function has been altered from what it was originally designed to be to a now fascinating historical oddity.

The same dynamic has occurred with the *lean* of the Catholic Church. There are those who like it, want to keep it, and even romantically defend it as it is. They see no need for a major foundational overhaul, for their present church suits their emotional, cultural, historical, and/or economic agendas. But, as in the case of the leaning tower, those functions represent an *alteration* from what the Church was intended to be, and our teaching will not have it so.

> Christ summons the Church, as she goes her pilgrim way, to that continual reformation of which she always has need, insofar as she is an institution of men here on earth (*Ecumenism*, 6).[5]

The Church was not created to be a crooked, bent, historical oddity used to gratify peoples' curiosities or agendas. No! Her Founder designed her to rise as a tall, strong, spiritual tower—a supernatural edifice capable of sounding a clarion call which summons people to a higher vision of eternally significant purposes, as well as warns them of imminent and perpetual danger.

First Proclamation

So the foundation upon which the Church is built (and rebuilt when necessary) is what the Bible calls the "gospel." As the Catholic Church teaches:

> The chief means of this implantation [of the Church] is the preaching of the gospel of Jesus Christ (*Decree on the Missionary Activity of the Church*, 6).[6]

But what do we mean by *gospel*? This is an important question because people who attend liturgical churches are already familiar with the term. If you were to ask such people, "Have you heard the gospel?" they would respond, "Of course I have. I hear it every Sunday." In their experience, "hearing the gospel" refers to that part of their church service in which a selection of Matthew, Mark, Luke, or John is proclaimed from the lectionary.

But in this context we are using the word in a different manner: we are referring to what St. Paul meant in such verses as Romans 1:16 where he stated, "I am not ashamed of the *gospel*. It is the power of God for the salvation of everyone who believes" (NAB, emphasis added). By this he could not have meant the words of one of the first four books of the New Testament—they weren't written yet! His term refers to the essential content to which every able person must freely respond in faith in order to enter a new relationship with God through Jesus Christ—salvation. It was the message he preached as he moved from town to town, establishing churches on Christ (cf. 1 Corinthians 3:10–11.) It is the *foundational* message, then, upon which the rest of Christianity is meant to be based, the only message by which the rest of Christianity makes sense:

> ...the kerygma, or gospel, is what gives origin to the Church... (Fr. Raniero Cantalamessa, preacher to the papal household, "Faith in Christ Today and at the Beginning of the Church," 2).[7]

For this reason, Catholic teaching employs another term, which differentiates that foundational message from the four Gospels—the *first proclamation*:

> This first proclamation is addressed specifically to those who have never heard the Good News of Jesus... (*On Evangelization*, 52).[8]

> ...the initial proclamation of the Gospel or missionary preaching to arouse faith... (*Catechism*, 6).[9]*

---

* Understandably, this can pose an initial confusion for those who associate the term *gospel* with only Matthew, Mark, Luke, or John. Questions may arise like, "What, then, is their place as 'gospels'?" and, "Why is the word *gospel* used for them?" The answer is that those four books attempt to take the foundational proclamation and expand on it. Scripture scholars agree that the core of the four gospels is the narration of Jesus' death, burial, and resurrection—the essence of the "first proclamation," as we will see in the next chapters. Each writer then wove other accounts into his basic story in order to invite the reader to meet and come to know the Jesus accepted by faith in the "first proclamation." This distinction is vital, especially today, because many who have read the gospels over the years have concluded that the content of the gospels is merely the teachings and personal example of Jesus of Nazareth. Jesus contributed something much more profound to humanity than simply showing us how to live, as we shall soon see.

This then is the "essential content, the living substance, which cannot be modified or ignored without seriously diluting the nature of evangelization itself" (*On Evangelization*, 25).[10] In other words, the foundation cannot be confused for that which is built upon it, nor can anything be substituted for it. Father Raniero Cantalamessa, "the Pope's preacher," stated it this way (emphasis added):

> The Churches with a strong dogmatic and theological tradition... run the risk of finding themselves at a disadvantage if *underneath* the immense heritage of doctrine, laws, and institutions, they do not find that primordial *nucleus capable of awakening faith by itself.*[11]

Other terms are used for the gospel or first proclamation. We have already been introduced to two of them used in Catholic and non-Catholic circles alike: "good news" is a literal rendering of the Greek compound word, *eu-angelion*, we normally translate as "gospel." Also, *kerygma* is a Greek term which means "proclamation," refers to this message, and is used mostly in theological circles. It has also been called the plan of salvation or the salvation message. Some, who explain its content by means of four propositions to be accepted in faith, call it the Four Spiritual Laws.

Call it what you will, we will now move on to the more important task of exploring the content of this message which has the power to transform humanity eternally; and as we do, we will demonstrate for all Bible-believing Christians just how common a heritage it is.

4

The Vision

In a speech delivered to the Harvard Law School Association of New York, the famous Supreme Court Justice Oliver Wendell Holmes, Jr. once said:

> I think it not improbable that man, like the grub that prepares a chamber for the winged things it never has seen but is to be—that man may have cosmic destinies that he does not understand.[1]

The good news of Christianity begins where Holmes left off. It not only affirms human life and its "cosmic destiny," but boldly reveals what our crowning purpose is. And though this vision of humans and humanity may not seem automatically evident to some, like even the grub, we have the capacity to intuit and be drawn toward it.

What is this *vision*? The Word of God tells us that we exist precisely because the greatest being that exists—God—created us. Our essence is that we are made in the nobility of His own image and likeness. He loves us and designed that we have an abundant and eternal life. Yet unmistakably as creatures, *life* and *fulfillment* consist of a relationship defined by loving deference to, and worship of, our Creator and of a relationship characterized by loving union with one another.

The *Catechism of the Catholic Church* teaches:

> God, infinitely perfect and blessed in himself,
> in a plan of sheer goodness freely created man
> to make him share in his own blessed life.[2]

> ...man is created by God and for God...[3]

These statements are certainly a mouthful. And they're loaded with implications that might be surprising, even for those who for years have considered themselves practicing Christians. Let's take a look at those implications.

JUST A RELIGION?

The first reality we find is that Christianity is quite unique among the systems of thought and belief that we call "religions." Since its central figure is identified as a personal being—and one who loves us, no less—Christianity cannot be viewed as an impersonal set of practices, guidelines, or laws. Some have even gone so far as to say that Christianity *isn't* a religion, it's a relationship. However we define it, one thing is clearly implied: God's purpose in creating us was not simply to get us to go through a set of motions we call "worship" or to follow a set of rules we call "commandments." No—He created us foremost to exist in *relationship* with Him: He, loving us first, and we, freely loving Him in return. Worship and obedience certainly have their place but only within this context. Outside of it, Christians become mere religious practitioners, who function more out of obligation to God than out of a completely free choice to enter into intimacy with Him. Indeed, some wish to maintain the comfortable distance possible for one who merely *pays dues* to God when required but never enters into real relationship.

I've heard some in my denomination even bristle at the term *personal relationship*, citing that those words aren't even found in the Bible.

They may not be found in the Bible, but they *are* found in the teaching of the Catholic Church, so no Catholic can bypass them. For example, the Vatican Council's *Decree on the Missionary Activity of the Church* speaks of being "led into the mystery of the love of God, who has called him [man] to enter a personal relationship with Him."[4] The *Catechism* states that the purpose of the mystery of faith is that people live "in a vital and personal relationship with the living and true God."[5]

Nor is this notion something new in the history of Christianity, even though the psychological vocabulary used to talk about personal relationship is. Historically, Catholic teaching has consistently pointed out that head knowledge of God or intellectual assent to the doctrines about God are not sufficient in order to live the Christian life. Consider the following:

> It is my opinion that our intellect does not have a natural power to be moved to the divine vision of Divinity (*Aescetical Homilies*).[6]
> —St. Isaac the Syrian, Seventh century

> For whoever believes, gives assent to the word of someone; thus, in any type of belief, it seems that the principal thing is the person to whose words the assent is given; those things through which one assents to that person are secondary (*Summa Theologica*).[7]
> —St. Thomas Aquinas, Thirteenth century

It is the proud, or rather foolish, men who examine the mysteries of faith which surpass all understanding with the faculties of the human mind, and rely on human reason which by the condition of man's nature, is weak and infirm (*Mirari Vos*).[8]

—POPE GREGORY XVI, NINETEENTH CENTURY

The faith is not only thought; it touches the whole being. Given that God made man with flesh and blood and entered into the tangible world, we have to try to encounter God with all the dimensions of our being (General Audience).[9]

—POPE BENEDICT XVI, TWENTY-FIRST CENTURY

In contemporary language, then, Christian religion is meant to be practiced only in the context of relationship with God. Without personal relationship, our religion is empty—and dead.

"TASTE AND SEE"

Personal relationship also implies personal relating, or what we might call "encounter" experiences. In the realm of the spiritual, then, (as Pope Benedict XVI asserted) we can and should have personal experiences of God in our relationship with Him. This is important to highlight because there are misconceptions of Christianity in which God is portrayed as beyond our contact, or as someone who does little we can actually experience in our lives right here and now.

You see, even among those who speak of "relationship" with God, the term can be used to mean something less than personal. In the natural realm, for example, it can be said that citizens of the United States have a relationship with the president: we are among those he governs, what he does affects us, and what we do can affect him. But as citizens, we don't expect to have consistent personal encounters or experiences with the president—it's not that *kind* of relationship. Yet this can describe how many relate to God. They might believe He knows us and even that there is some kind of invisible grace emanating from Him to us; but many do not expect to experience Him, especially to the extent that it would make a serious difference in life this side of the grave.

Such a view of Christianity less resembles the vision of God in the scriptures than it does the ancient philosophy of Stoicism. It was from Stoicism that we derived our term *stoic*, unaffected by joy or pain. Unfortunately, many imagine a God who is exactly that—detached from our delights and our sorrows. It is easy to see how religion can then be reduced to a set of head propositions to be believed and a set of disagreeable obligations to be gotten out of the way. Consequently, assuming that this is "as good as it gets" with God, people then adjust their lives accordingly, trying to find joy and meaning of life elsewhere.

This view also resembles the image of God advanced by philosophers of the Enlightenment (the eighteenth century Western European movement which formulated much of our scientific approach today)—and it was to this image that Pope John Paul II responded, "*No, absolutely not!* God is not someone who remains only outside of the world, content to be in Himself all-knowing and omnipotent."[10]

Such misconceptions about who God is explain why people might shrink from taking God seriously, much less seeing Him as the center of their existence. The initial proposition of the gospel crashes through that religious *glaze over* with the good news that not only *can* we experience God and His love, but we are *meant* to, *supposed* to, within a personal relationship.

And this is by no means a Christian invention. Jewish religion (out of which Christianity was birthed) distinguished itself among other pagan religions by its metaphor of "covenant." A covenant was an agreement among people to enter into a particular kind of *relating* to one another (marriage, for example). Jewish religion was comfortable borrowing analogies from human life experience to express what a connection with God was all about; and for them, the human dynamics of a covenant seemed to supply the most comprehensive terms of that connection. Israel even went so far as to declare that a covenant was God's idea and initiative in the first place. So, whereas pagan religion stressed one-sided obligations, duties, and sacrifices in order to even approach their gods, Israelites dared to assert that, while not being on an equal status with Him, their God also bound Himself to relate to them. Thus, the Jewish connection with God was not like that found in pagan religions—a distant or merely ritualistic sort of relating, it was *covenantal* religion. As a matter of fact, Jews claimed that their bond with God was akin to a marriage: He *loved* them. Thus, their covenant was even characterized by the degree of mutuality and intimacy that today we would properly call *personal relationship*.

We have already said that the essence of a personal relationship is humans encountering and experiencing one another. By analogy, then, biblical religion implies the same about relating to God. Again, the exact words *encounter* and *experience* are not found in the pages of the Bible. But the concepts are. For example, both Testaments are filled with stories of people interacting with God in very substantial experiences. In the same vein, the writer of Psalm 34 invites listeners to "taste and see" how good the Lord is (v. 8). Using a very experiential metaphor, people are invited to make relating to the Lord as real as enjoying a good meal. You can't get more experiential than that! Also, the Hebrew verb "to know" is the equivalent of what we mean by "to experience"—yet another reason why contemporary people in the Western world miss the biblical emphasis on experiencing God. We use the word *know* to denote the conclusion of an intellectual process: to *know* something is to have tried and succeeded in understanding it to be true. ("I know that," means that I've learned something about that.) But in the Middle Eastern mindset, "to know" was to have an experiential encounter. For example, what Mary said in Luke 1:34 to express her surprise at the angel Gabriel's annunciation, literally means in the original Greek, "How can this be, since I do not know man?" In other words, "How can I bear a child when I have not had the proper *experiential encounter* with a man in order to conceive a child?" We don't use the word *know* in such a way, and Mary's expression literally translated would confuse us without this explanation. So, whereas we might think that *knowing God* amounts to little more than affirming the correct *facts* about Him, the Hebrew mindset connects knowing God not with abstract thinking, but with an experiential encounter which reveals something about Him. It's the difference between knowing *about* someone, and really knowing that individual personally. Or, it's like recognizing that I can't know what it's like to skydive or to drive a car, if I've never had these experiences. Reading all the books in the world about those activities is no substitute for the experience itself—and we certainly wouldn't want anyone *teaching* us these activities with only a book-reader's knowledge. So, too, Christianity which is born out of the good news subordinates head knowledge of God to an experiential knowledge of God. The first without the second is ultimately empty.

And Catholic sources substantiate this. Among the varied citations, for example, an early Church father, whom historians call Pseudo-Dionysius, recorded that his mentor knew spiritual realities not just from learning about them, but by experiencing them.[11] St. Benedict of Aniane (mid eighth to ninth centuries) stated, "No one is made a friend of God except by the knowledge of experiencing [literally: 'of tasting']."[12] St. Thomas Aquinas, though a prominent medieval *thinker*, declared that "our intellect, as it is in this life, does not know Him [God] as He is."[13] And as late as 1979, John Paul II felt a need to call attention to the fact that a certain number of young people come to churches for formation in Christianity "without receiving any other initiation into the faith and still without any explicit personal attachment to Jesus Christ."[14] His concern was that Christian formation had become devoid of what constitutes initiation into the faith—an explicit relationship which is *real* in experience.

The teaching is clear. It does not say that having a religious experience is the goal of Christianity or that every religious experience is authentically Christian. Experience must line up with what is revealed by God in His Word. Nevertheless, experience of God in a personal relationship with Him is an essential ingredient of normal Christianity.

"How Good the Lord Is"

What makes the good news so good is that it invites us to "taste and see" that God is 100 percent good and 100 percent loving. And this is no small thing! For, by definition, God is the highest and greatest being in existence, and therefore, a being that, by nature, can both elicit feelings of intimidation in us and overwhelm us. Indeed, popular misconceptions by everyone from comedians to churchgoers have created an image of God of raw, unchecked power with a fickle and volatile disposition—much like the gods of mythology. No wonder atheism seems to be such a viable option for people today.

It is for this reason that Catholic teaching states (emphasis added):

> It is not superfluous to...bear witness that in
> his Son God has *loved* the world—that in his
> Incarnate Word he has given being to all things
> and has called men to eternal life (*On Evange-
> lization*, 26).[15]

The good news is that one does not need to cower before the Divine in fear, as is the case in so many other religious systems. God is as approachable as love itself; and being that His relationship to the world is defined by love, He can fulfill the greatest desire of the human heart—the experiential ability of each individual to say, "I am loved by the greatest being that exists, the One to whom all are accountable, the One who defines reality itself, and therefore *I am loveable!*"

Nor does one have to earn God's love:

> In the course of its history, Israel was able to
> discover that God had only one reason to reveal
> himself to them...his sheer gratuitous love (cf.
> Deut. 4:37; 7:8; 10:15)" (*Catechism*, 218).[16]

Webster's defines *gratuitous* as "given freely, without recompense, or regardless of merit; not called for by the circumstances;

unwarranted." We don't have to work for it; we can't deserve it. Another word to use is *unconditional.* God simply loves us— whatever our condition, regardless of our response. And as long as we are on this planet, nothing can change that reality. Now I ask you: for persons who believe in God, is that good news, or what? And for those who don't, might this not persuade them to reconsider their position?

THE GOSPEL VISION

So, to put it all together, the gospel calls out to humans of every generation and declares that God exists; and out of love alone, He created us with a purpose, plan, and destiny—namely to live a full, abundant, and eternal life, a life as every human being deep down really wants to live. And it is precisely through a relationship with Him that we uncover and live this plan. Far from being a boring or capricious deity whose pleasure is to snuff out human fulfillment, God's agenda is to provide us with a life that anyone in his or her right mind would want to live forever. That's why it's called "eternal."

I know of a brilliant, energetic, young Evangelical pastor who attempted to find out why people in this country were statistically checking out of church attendance ever since the early 1960s. To do so, he followed some common-sense inner leads, and simply interviewed a sizable number of households in his area over a period of weeks about this issue. Sad to say, his data revealed a frequent response of non-church-attenders: going to church was an experience that did not relate to the daily needs, concerns, and pains of their lives; in short, the Church was irrelevant. *Irrelevant.*

In a 1998 visit to a local parish in Rome, Pope John Paul II had a similar reflection on his own worldwide sphere:

When we study baptism, when we administer this principal sacrament of our faith, and when we read the words of St. Paul to the Romans, we see more clearly that the present practice has become increasingly insufficient and superficial.[17]

The gospel's first Spiritual Truth asserts that religion without relationship *is* irrelevant, but God is not. Either God is relevant to every person's real lived life, or He's not God at all. Oliver Wendell Holmes had more than a clue: every person *does* "have cosmic desires that he does not understand,"[18] and the God of unconditional love eagerly awaits us to discover them.

5

THE PROBLEM

OST OF US have at least heard of the film *The Matrix*, starring Keanu Reeves. In this futuristic, science-fiction thriller, the world is taken over by computers. But true to sci-fi form, these are no ordinary computers—they need the energy of human bodies to survive. Accordingly, the master machines keep a supply of genetically engineered humans whom they permanently anesthetize. The *matrix*, then, is the created imaginary world in which these humans can think they are alive, conscious, and involved in everyday normal activities, when in reality they are still blinded to the truth about themselves and thus able to be kept in bondage to the way things really are.

A group of rebels, however, breaks free of the matrix. Led by a character named Morpheus, they begin living an alternative reality and become the quarry of cyber cops. In the process they meet Keanu Reeves' character, Neo, and discover that he is the one prophesied to liberate people from the matrix.

Earlier, Neo had begun to awaken to the truth himself; while living in the illusionary matrix, he began to experience doubts he couldn't explain but which were, nevertheless, real. When Neo finally meets the rebels, Morpheus discerns the cause of Neo's splintered mind and offers to initiate him into the full truth that Neo has heretofore only sensed. The leader gives him the choice of two pills: one would tranquilize the pain created by the inner instincts and transition Neo comfortably back into the matrix; the other, should he have the courage to take it, would open his eyes to the truth and give him a place in the *alternate* yet actual reality.

The second Spiritual Truth introduces us to the fact that we are all caught in a *matrix*. Even though God loves us, our lives and the world are no longer what He originally intended them to be. By a tragic choice we humans made, creation has been taken over by a dark spiritual entity which has put us in a *force field* contrary to God's design for us. And this matrix is so strong that it even deceives us into thinking that the way we live is normal, when in actuality we are both blind to the truth about ourselves and kept in the painful bondage of our unreality—all without even knowing it!

Now for many, that's "a hard pill to swallow." Certainly we live in an age that would love the message of Christianity to proceed no further than the last chapter. In the belief system of many—including those systems cloaking themselves in Christianity—we're "home safe," spiritually speaking, once we grasp that God loves us. The appeal of this type of theology, no doubt, is that it feels good. But it is identical to the first choice Morpheus offered Neo—a pleasant analgesic that blurs the pain of our true condition and actually thrusts us back into a comatose matrix of unreality that holds us captive. Only the invitation to an *alternate* reality, which exposes how much bondage we are really in, can liberate us from this matrix. That is why the good news which Evangelicals and Catholics propagate cannot be complete without visiting some notions which our culture readily dismisses as archaic: sin, judgment, the need to be made right with God, and, yes, even hell.

Is Sin Catholic?

It may be that in the experience of many, Catholics just don't talk about sin any more. Before the Vatican Council, this was certainly not the case. (My now-deceased aunt used to tell me, "When we grew up Catholic, *everything* was a sin!") In an effort to gain balance, however, the pendulum swung quite to the other extreme, and many Catholics joined the ranks of those who call themselves Christians but really don't reflect often on the reality of sin in their lives. This syndrome, I believe, is what prompted the mental health professional Karl Menninger to write the book *Whatever Became of Sin?* detailing the devastating effects such a state can have on the human psyche.

One thing that *didn't* become of sin was that it was disposed of in official Catholic teachings. Even a brief survey of the documents of the Vatican II will uncover its comprehensive grasp of the reality and effects of sin. The Vatican Council itself—which is often blamed for the popular Catholic de-emphasis of sin—in reality, had a lot to say about the subject. For example, the *Declaration on the Relationship of the Church to Non-Christian Religions* lists sin as one of the profound riddles of the human condition about which we look for answers.[1] The *Pastoral Constitution on the Church in the Modern World*, which sought to recast the Catholic Church in terms which would be taken seriously in contemporary life, proffered perhaps the Council's greatest amount and depth of insight into sin. Witness this bold statement:

> Examining his heart, man finds that he has inclinations toward evil too, and is engulfed by manifold ills which cannot come from his good Creator.[2]

According to this assertion, sin *is* real on planet earth. So real that other sections of the same document go on to specify some of its effects: "bondage,"[3] a humanity which is "fallen"[4] and which now possesses an intelligence whose "certitude is partly obscured,"[5] and the ability to create "a conscience which by degrees grows practically sightless."[6] The Council's *Decree on the Apostolate of the Laity* states that because of sin,

> ...men have frequently fallen into multiple errors concerning the true God, the nature of men, and the principles of the moral law.[7]

Catholic teaching spells out even more about sin than how it affects the individual. Though "sin is a personal act" (*Catechism*, 1868)[8] it is of sin's nature that it poses a problem to more than just the one who commits it. The Introduction to the Rite of Penance (confession) states:

> The hidden and gracious mystery of God unites us all through a supernatural bond: on this basis one person's sin harms the rest...[9]

This statement obviously applies to personal sin which directly causes harm to others. But an even more profound reality is implied here: in that "sin is before all else an offense toward God, a rupture of communion with him" (*Catechism*, 1440)[10] it is essentially spiritual in nature; thus personal sin, even when it directly affects no one, proliferates the darkness of the world, and in doing so, still affects its inhabitants. This is what the *Catechism* so aptly names "our interdependence in the drama of sin."[11]

This interdependence manifests itself very concretely in "communal situations and social structures that are the fruit

of men's sins (Cf. John Paul II, *Reconciliation and Penance* 16)"
(*Catechism*, 408)[12] for:

> Sins give rise to social situations and institu-
> tions that are contrary to the divine goodness.
> "Structures of sin" are the expression and effect
> of personal sins (*Catechism*, 1869).[13]

What's more, sin's effects pertain not only to our human relationships. Catholic teaching even takes note of the "cosmic"
dimensions by this statement summarizing the full sweep of
sin's influence:

> At the same time he [man] became out of harmony
> with himself, with others, and with all created
> things (*Church in the Modern World*, 13).[14]

So, the teaching of the Catholic Church does not shy away
from speaking about sin. Sin is part of divine revelation,
without which we "are tempted to explain it [sin] as merely a
developmental flaw, a psychological weakness, a mistake, or the
necessary consequence of an inadequate social structure, etc."
(*Catechism*, 387).[15] No!

> Sin is present in human history; any attempt
> to ignore it or to give this dark reality other
> names would be futile (*Catechism*, 386).[16]

> Like a physician who probes the wound before
> treating it, God, by His Word and by His Spirit,
> casts a living light on sin... (*Catechism*, 1848).[17]

In an interview, John Paul II shared candidly on his own
commitment to do exactly that in God's name:

> This is another point that is absolutely unac-
> ceptable to post-Enlightenment thought....*It
> refuses to accept the reality of sin*....the Pope
> becomes *persona non grata* when he tries to
> convince the world of human sin.[18]

Let there be no doubt that if Catholics ignore the reality of
sin, they do so outside of their own Church's tradition.

But There's More

The gospel not only names sin a reality, it shows us the exact
nature and scope of its power in the *matrix*. Why is this so important to know? Because there *are* those who would not deny
sin's reality, but who erroneously believe they can take care
of the problem through the proper equation of human effort
and God's grace. However, the gospel, and Catholic teaching,
proclaims that the force field of sin is a lot stronger than we
imagine. Every sin, no matter how mortal or venial, is but a
symptom of a deeper dilemma: every sinful action originates
with a human heart that in some way desires rebellion and
independence from God. *That's* the real problem.

> Although he was made by God in a state of
> holiness, from the very dawn of history man
> abused his liberty, at the urging of personified
> Evil. Man set himself against God and sought
> to find fulfillment apart from God (*Church in
> the Modern World*, 13).[19]

> Sin sets itself against God's love for us and turns
> our hearts away from it. Like the first sin, it is
> disobedience, a revolt against God through the

will to become "like gods" (Gen. 3:5)... (*Catechism*, 1850).[20]

Rebellion. Independence. That's the *real* sin. As a matter of fact, that's the *only* sin, and it manifests itself in the countless ways we call our sins.

The Catholic Church's teaching is also clear on the forceful nature of sin: it's "the gift that keeps on giving."

> Sin creates a proclivity to sin... (*Catechism*, 1865).[21]

And so,

> This results in perverse inclinations which cloud conscience and corrupt the concrete judgment of good and evil (*Catechism*, 1865).[22]

In other words, sin places us in a state in which we have lost the natural ability to even recognize life as God intended it to be (life without sin). That is why most people think themselves basically OK as they are and go about their business as if there was really nothing radically subnormal about their lives. We are caught in *the matrix*.

THE STRUGGLE BEGINS

Like Neo, however, there are those who begin to awaken to the truth. In this matrix of sin, the awakening manifests itself in anything from a vague moral discomfort, to an awareness of the moral guilt of specific sins, to a full-blown self-indictment about one's rebellion and independence before God.

Yet, this is but the beginning of the struggle, for it is at this stage that humans can want to fix their troubled heart through the equation I mentioned earlier. Here it is that people believe: If I just tried harder, did more good works, went to church, went to church more often, prayed, prayed more, read the Bible, employed religious rituals, frequented the sacraments, frequented them more often, etc., etc., etc., I could make myself right with God. Life—and even religion—then becomes a quest for the correct formula, the proper combination of variables, which will render the human soul at peace with the Divine. Even psychology gets in on the act. Where it seems the real sting of sin cannot be relativized, one can still believe what humanism tells us: I'm OK, you're OK. Yes, there are those who sincerely trust that some combination of the above methods is the ticket to right relationship with God. But the Catholic Church teaches otherwise.

> [Persons] are incapable of...meriting their justification before God or of attaining salvation by their own abilities (*Joint Declaration*, 19).[23]

> The universal design for the salvation of the human race is not...achieved merely through those multiple endeavors, including religious ones, by which men search for God... (*Missionary Activity*, 3).[24]

In other words, we can't make ourselves right with God—even by practicing religion.

Now some would respond, "Who says we have to be completely right before Him?" It is a popular belief that because God is loving, either He "grades on a curve" when it comes to our righteousness (after all, we're only human) or somehow in the end He'll let us slip by (do your best and He'll understand the rest). But this is not what the Word of God, or the Catholic Church, teaches.

> The Law indeed makes up one inseparable whole, and St. James recalls, "Whoever keeps the whole law but fails in one point has become guilty of all of it" (James 2:10; cf. Gal. 3:10; 5:3) (*Catechism*, 578).[25*]

That means God overlooks *no* violation of His will. He will not designate certain parts of His Law that we'll be allowed to bypass by invoking a personal *human-weakness* exemption.

"But I go to confession," many Catholics would say. Does going to confession make us capable of fulfilling the entire law? Does it erase what we've shown causes all sin in the first place—rebellion and independence before God? Can anyone ever say, "Thank God! Now that I've gone to confession I'm capable of keeping His whole Law without failure; like Jesus, my every thought and emotion is lined up with God's will such that now I will not fail in one point"? Obviously not!

But, if not, then everybody who trusts in that sacrament to make them right with God will find their rebellion and independence still unaccounted for and will still have to worry about what James and the *Catechism* call being "guilty of it all [i.e., the whole Law]." In light of this, going to confession, and all other popular assurances of right standing with God, simply crumble. So much for, "But I'm really a good person," or "I know I'm a sin-

---

* Galatians 3:10 says, "On the other hand, those who rely on the keeping of the Law are under a curse, since Scripture says, '*Cursed be everyone who does not persevere in observing <u>everything</u> prescribed in the book of the Law*'" (underlined emphasis added). Paul argues that anyone who appeals to the fact that he or she observes an adequate percentage of God's commands and is therefore right with Him, is fooling himself. God determines what is acceptable, not us, and He *has* communicated His standard: the very law to which the person appeals for his or her righteousness condemns anyone who does not fulfill it perfectly. As unreasonable as this sounds to us, it makes perfect sense. God's nature is Holy. He can have no fellowship with sin on any level without changing what makes Him God.

ner, but at least I'm not _____!" (Fill in the blank with your favorite notorious criminal.) And the list goes on.

The gospel asserts not only that we are sinners and need to be made right with God at the very deepest level, but that there is no human means of doing so—not even religious works. The problem is not only sin itself, but the fact that we are *powerless* over it and over the broken relationship with God which it causes.

> ...the control of the soul's spiritual faculties over the body is shattered... (*Catechism*, 400).[26]

> Therefore man is split within himself....Indeed, man finds that by himself he is incapable of battling the assaults of evil successfully, so that everyone feels as though he is bound in chains (*Church in the Modern World*, 13).[27]

> ...for "all have sinned and have need of the glory of God" (Rom. 3:23). By himself and by his own power, no one is freed from sin or raised above himself, or completely rid of...his servitude (*Missionary Activity*, 8).[28]

The only way out of this dilemma is by some means other than human power, even if we are aided by grace.* We need God to do something for us that we *can't* do for ourselves: we need Him to *save* us. When it comes to sin, our necessity is not only divine help, assistance, guidance, or advice; we need divine *salvation*.

---

* The heresy of Pelagianism in the early Church claimed that we have the capacity to save ourselves from the effects of sin by the exercise of our free will. Many today still view the Christian life in exactly the same way—we need God's *help*, but we basically do the work ourselves.

...the Church has a single intention: that God's Kingdom may come, and that the *salvation* of the whole human race may come to pass (*Church in the Modern World*, 45),[29] (emphasis added).

As the kernel and center of His Good News, Christ proclaims *salvation*, this great gift of God which is liberation from everything that oppresses man, but which is above all liberation from sin and the Evil One... (*On Evangelization*, 9),[30] (emphasis added).

He [Jesus] went further by proclaiming before the Pharisees that, since sin is universal, those who pretend not to need salvation are blind to themselves (cf. John 8:33–36; 9:40–41). (*Catechism*, 588)[31]

So, let's summarize. Our sin is real. It lies at the very core of our being and it cannot be *adjusted* out of us by any human means or by the practice of religion; yet, it must be dealt with if we are to be free from its curse and restored to fellowship with God. What it takes, then, is a *Savior*—one who is capable of conquering that root problem within us and finally making us right with God.

And, the good news is that a Savior is precisely what God has given us. For those who are seeking, there *is* a way out of *the matrix*. Read on.

6

THE SOLUTION

HUMANISTS WOULD CALL Him a great teacher. Eastern religions and New Age enthusiasts say He's a high-ranking spiritual guru type who imparted mystical enlightenment. Psychologists identify Him as a self-actualized man whose example can bring us into interior integration. Activists would celebrate Him as the ultimate radical who led a social revolution. Devotees of *The Da Vinci Code* tell us He was a controversial figure who, if He returned today, would debunk the claims of His followers. Muslims regard Him as a major prophet. Many people have many things to say about *Jesus of Nazareth*.

But Christianity says He is nothing less than the *Savior of the entire human race.* Teachers have come and gone. Spiritual masters have come and gone. Inspirational figures have come and gone, as have social revolutionaries, influential religious leaders, and humans who left a legacy of lives worth imitating. But Jesus of Nazareth did something that none of these has done, because Jesus of Nazareth was someone that none of these was: He was—and still is—the Savior of the world.

When I was in high school, the rock opera *Jesus Christ Superstar* made its debut. And that was perfect timing for me, because just then I started asking the questions posed by its theme song: "Jesus Christ, Jesus Christ. Who are you? What have you sacrificed?" From New Testament times on, people's imaginations have engaged in answering those questions. Works like *The Gospel of Judas* have alerted us to the fact that, from the beginning, many things were written about Jesus, even in "gospels" other than those we find in the Bible. The modern mind yet continues to wrestle with the meaning of His presence on earth. Everything from Nikos Kazantzakis' *The Last Temptation of Christ* to Dan Brown's *The Da Vinci Code* has presented interpretations of the personhood of Jesus Christ and His relevance to humanity. But what are we to make of these presentations, some of which seem quite fanciful? How is one to sort through all that's written in order to discern some semblance of truth? It certainly seems there could be endless possibilities of what to believe.

Yet when one takes seriously and actually studies Scripture (and in the case of Catholics, even our teaching), quite a defined picture emerges. And so, even though Andrew Lloyd Webber's cry first surfaced in musical forms which today may seem dated, an essential part of Christianity's gospel is to tackle those searching questions he posed: Who is Jesus Christ? And, What is His sacrificial death on the cross all about? This chapter will present Christianity's answers.

An Outstanding Claim

Evangelization will also always contain—as the foundation, center and at the same time summit of its dynamism—a clear proclamation that, in Jesus Christ, the Son of God made man, who died and rose from the dead, salvation is offered to all men, as a gift of God's grace and mercy (*On Evangelization*, 27).[1]

If by some stroke of genius, medical researchers were able to find the cure for cancer, the discovery would be hailed as possibly the greatest contribution of science to this era. The treatment would be heralded from east to west, and its discoverers would gain international renown.

In a similar vein, Christianity makes a claim which is nothing short of astounding: there is a cure for the "cancer" of sin which we spoke about so explicitly in the last chapter—and His name is Jesus.

One day as I was driving along the expressway, my attention caught a billboard displaying the words, "We will never stop trying." Next to the words was a child who was obviously sick. Another glance told me that this was an advertisement for a children's research hospital committed to finding a cure for cancer on behalf of its young victims. Even in the few seconds I was able to view the billboard, my heart was touched, as most hearts would be.

Similarly, the moving message of Christianity is that, even though the cancer of sin was brought on by our own choices, humans are still God's creations—His "kids," whose suffering touched His heart, and to whom He was committed to uncover "the cure" for sin. Thereby, in the Old Testament He established relationship in His covenants, then revealed right from wrong in His Law, and later even appealed for repentance through His prophets. However, though these were all acts of grace on God's part, none of them *worked*—our sin remained. Still, He "never stopped trying," until He revealed the perfect cure—Jesus.

But how can we make these bold assertions with integrity? What, exactly, do we believe Jesus did to cure our sin disease? We've already referenced at the beginning of this chapter that people have many things to say about Jesus' identity—so do they also, about what He did to save us. Some would state, "He taught us how to live," or "He gave us an example of perfect, unselfish love." Others might say, "He challenged and changed the way society is to operate," or "He brought peace to the individual heart through His unconditional love and His forgiveness."

All these, of course, are true. But, in defining Jesus' saving work, these statements are nearsighted. There is a popular utilitarian view that perceives religion as just one force among others which can improve life. This is why people so readily believe that "one religion is just as good as another" as long as they all meet the common goal—what we regard to be human betterment. This position, however, represents more the deism of the Enlightenment era than it does Christianity. For example, an Enlightenment philosopher, David Hume, states in his work *Dialogues Concerning Natural Religion*, "the proper office of religion is to regulate the heart of men, humanize their conduct, infuse the spirit of temperance, order and obedience."[2]* Christianity certainly affirms that individuals, groups, and societies are bettered by the teaching and example of Jesus of Nazareth. But it doesn't stop there in defining His saving work:

> The Paschal mystery of Christ's cross and Resurrection stands at the center of the Good News that the apostles, and the Church following them, are to proclaim to the world (*Catechism*, 571).[3]

For the Catholic Church defines salvation as:

> ...this great gift of God which is liberation from everything that oppresses man but which

---

* Other examples include George Washington's farewell address of 1796: "Of all the dispositions and habits which lead to political prosperity, religion and morality are indispensable supports." Note the subordination of religion to the main focus (political prosperity), and that the term religion is unspecified.

is above all liberation from sin and the Evil One... (*On Evangelization*, 9).[4]

Now, I submit this towering objective cannot be accomplished by mere teaching or *enlightenment* as some propose. Neither will it happen by social or political change alone nor by someone setting an example to follow—even if it's a perfect one. Neither will divine forgiveness of individual transgressions effect this change. (The people of the Old Testament already had access to this.) No—sin has enslaved humanity into a cosmic matrix—a force field controlled by a dark power which must be overcome in order for us (who have cooperated with it and are now by nature powerless over it) to be liberated.

This is exactly what Jesus did to save humanity. By taking the cosmic consequences of all sin into Himself on the cross, by offering Himself there to be the victim of our sin choice, by standing in our place there and taking the full "rap" of our sin's effects *for* us, and by offering Himself there as a ransom so that the just punishment of our sin could still be fulfilled, Jesus opened the door for anyone who desires to go free.

> By his obedience unto death, Jesus accomplished the substitution of the suffering Servant, who "makes himself an *offering for sin*," when "he bore the sin of many," and who "shall make many to be accounted righteous" for "he shall bear their iniquities" (Isa. 53:10–12). Jesus atoned for our faults and made satisfaction for our sins to the Father (cf. Council of Trent [1547]: DS 1529). It is love "to the end" (John 13:1) that confers on Christ's sacrifice its value

as redemption and reparation, as atonement and satisfaction (*Catechism*, 615–616).[5]

That act, and that act alone, released us from the hold of sin and gave us the way out of the *matrix*. This fact was confirmed by Jesus' resurrection, which finally manifested what His cross accomplished—complete authority of unimaginable cosmic proportions, over any dominion of sin in us, up to and including death itself. Thus,

> All this [salvation] is…definitively accomplished by his death and resurrection (*On Evangelization*, 9).[6]

> God's saving plan was accomplished 'once for all' (Heb. 9:26) by the redemptive death of his Son Jesus Christ (*Catechism*, 571).[7]

THE WAY OUT

It sounds grand. But what specifically does that mean? What does this liberation actually look like? Many make the mistake of thinking that salvation amounts to nothing more than a pre-dated ticket to heaven. On the contrary, there are three effects we begin to experience *now*.

First, because Jesus took our sin into Himself and paid the debt we owe, it is now possible that an individual can be made right with God again, not based on his of her own merits and what he or she has done, but based on what *Jesus* did. This is what Christianity calls "justification"—being OK with God because the sin problem has been properly settled by His appointed Savior, who fulfilled His appointed plan.

> Justification is at the same time *the acceptance of God's righteousness* through faith in Jesus Christ (*Catechism*, 1991).[8]

> By grace alone, in faith in Christ's saving work and not because of any merit on our part, we are accepted by God... (*Joint Declaration*, 15).[9]

So we can say that because of Jesus' cross and resurrection a person's sin debt can be cancelled. And this leads us to the second effect of salvation, for part of the debt of sin is *servitude* to it. But, because Jesus won and manifested victory over sin and all its effects, because He satisfied the just demand for punishment of our sin, He now has the right to set anyone free from enslavement to it.

> Salvation not only confronts evil in each of its existing forms in this world but proclaims *victory over evil* (*Crossing*, 21).[10]

In other words, He can declare that sin no longer has the license to hold you or me bound to serve it. He can actually command sin to release its grip on us once and for all, if that's what we really want. And even though some of those old sin patterns may take awhile to disappear, sin will not ultimately govern us as it used to; the root rebellion and independence before God, which formerly controlled our lives, will no longer be able to dominate us—down to the core of our beings, we *can* be changed. The U.S. Conference of Catholic Bishops, in its concern that this part of the gospel be kept clear in doctrine, wrote:

Instruction must remind the student of the
sufferings and the death on the cross which
Christ endured to destroy the effects of sin.[11]

Thus the second benefit of being saved by Jesus is that He
can destroy the effects of sin in our lives—some immediately,
some over time, but *all* starting right here and now.

Summarizing this point and introducing our third, *Catechism of the Catholic Church* says:

The Paschal mystery has two aspects: by his
death, Christ liberates us from sin; by his Resurrection, he opens for us the way to a new life.[12]

Christianity asserts that Jesus can offer us nothing less than
a brand new life. How else can we describe the state of a person
who has been liberated from the power of sin and made right
with God?

Just as when Jesus died, He died *for us*, so too, when He rose
(manifesting the victory of His death) He rose *for us*. In other
words, He not only wants to share with us the fruits of His triumph over sin, He also wants to share with us the new resurrected
life which comes with that achievement. So the gift of salvation
includes not only a right standing with God, a freedom from and
power over sin, but the very eternal, resurrected life of Jesus within. This makes the recipient nothing less than a new creation.

This union of Christ with man is in itself a
mystery. From the mystery is born "the new
man" called to become a partaker of God's
life... (*The Redeemer of Humanity*, 18).[13]

This new reality which takes up residence inside a saved person, this new life, is the person of the Holy Spirit—prophesied in the Old Testament as part of God's blueprint of salvation and released by virtue of Jesus' cross and resurrection.

> Now can this divine plan, accomplished in Christ, the firstborn and head of the new creation, be embodied in mankind by the outpouring of the Spirit... (*Catechism*, 686).[14]

The new life will manifest itself in a number of ways. One thing the Holy Spirit will do is to transform the very desires of our hearts and progressively bring them into conformity with God's will. Then, He will also give us the power we need to obey God. This is noteworthy. You see, most religions define how they think their adherents ought to live life; Christianity, however, is the only religion which teaches what its divine being desires of us, and then gives us the power to do it.

Not to say there won't be struggle in some areas of our lives. But the struggle is now one of learning to submit to the Holy Spirit's powerful operation through faith, not one of striving to obey God by our own willpower. And thus, because the Spirit is Jesus' own resurrected existence, the new life also becomes an experience in which Jesus literally lives His life in us. In Galatians 2:20, one of the scriptures in the regular cycle of readings in the Latin Rite Catholic liturgy, Paul tells us that the life which Christians live is not our own—it is Christ's life living in us. The Catholic Church's teaching puts it this way:

> The Christian man, conformed to the likeness of that Son who is the firstborn of many brothers, receives "the first-fruits of the Spirit" (Rom. 8:23)

by which he becomes capable of discharging the
new law of love (*Church in the Modern World*,
22).[15]

Grace is a *participation in the life of God*
(*Catechism*, 1997).[16]

Finally, the new life is so full that it will overflow in humanly
extraordinary manifestations which we can only conclude come
from God.

> ...grace also includes the gifts that the Spirit
> grants us to associate with his work.... There
> are furthermore *special graces*, also called
> *charisms*...such as the gift of miracles...
> (*Catechism*, 2003).[17]

And so, "new life" is not just a phrase for a banner with but-
terflies and flowers at Easter time. While no community we
would call Christian denies Jesus the title, *Savior*, still, huge
segments of the Church world have reduced to a mere cliché
this profound accomplishment of Jesus *as* Savior. Even though
Catholic teaching calls people who receive Jesus' salvation,
"those whose life has been transformed" (*On Evangelization*,
23),[18] in my experience the majority who say they're Catholic
don't actually *expect* that being a Christian will amount to a
quantum-leap change in their real-lived lives, much less one that
can only be described as "new creation"—even though our own
Church teaches these things. The modern person in general can
hardly believe that a historical event some two thousand years
ago—the death and resurrection of Jesus—radically altered the
possibilities of human existence both now and for all eternity.
Yet, this is exactly what Christianity unashamedly claims.

No Other Name

Because of the unparalleled effects of the cross and resurrection of Jesus of Nazareth, the gospel makes yet another unprecedented claim. It holds that Jesus is not only *a* savior, but *the* Savior—the *sole* Savior of the entire human race, of every time, of every place—Jesus alone.

Now I imagine that statement just raised some eyebrows, both Catholic and Evangelical. And I can understand why. Regretfully, all kinds of salvation systems have been preached across Catholic pulpits and podiums. Many of them would harmonize under the popular "There are many, many ways to God" slogan. But official Catholic teaching would not affirm such unqualified statements.

> If we go back to the beginnings of the Church we find a clear affirmation that Christ is the one Savior of all, the only one able to reveal God and lead to God....For all people—Jews and Gentiles alike—salvation can only come from Jesus Christ (*The Mission*, 5).[19]

> In this sense, one can and must say that Jesus Christ has a significance and value for the human race and its history, which are unique and singular, proper to him alone, exclusive, universal, and absolute. Jesus is, in fact, the Word of God made man for the salvation of all (*Salvific Universality*, 15).[20]

How could Christianity make such bold assertions? The answer is actually quite simple. No other human has ever claimed to do what we have stated that Jesus did. That's because no other human has ever done what Jesus did for the salvation of the world. John Paul II described it as,

> ...that unique and irreversible restoration of man and the world to the Father that was carried out once for all by him... (*The Redeemer*, 20).[21]

If a person assents to these propositions, the conclusion that Jesus is the only Savior of the world is mere logic—no less logical than when one day we might be able to say, "Since John Doe was the only one who discovered the surefire cure for cancer, no one else did."

And the reason no one else has ever claimed what Jesus accomplished is that no one else *could* do what He did. Thus,

> No man, not even the holiest, was ever able to take on himself the sins of all men and offer himself as a sacrifice for all (*Catechism*, 616).[22]

Yes, some guru-types have claimed to have reached complete perfection; but the only human who ever possessed and maintained a sinless nature such that He never needed personal salvation from sin, was Jesus. Thereby only He could offer Himself as a perfect and just ransom for the sin of humanity.

> ...Christ does not resemble Muhammad or Socrates or Buddha. *He is totally original and unique* (*Crossing*, 45).[23]

"Then where *does* that leave other religions?" you might ask. It certainly disqualifies any other religious founder or figure from being able to save humanity from sin. However, there are two possible answers to the question, each depending on the concern of those asking. Some may ask because they are at least inclined to believe what biblical Christianity teaches about Jesus, yet are honestly troubled about the implications for those who have not yet heard. And to them we would respond with Jesus' own urgent words in Mark 16:15 and parallel passages—Christians *must* share the gospel with every living creature. Beyond what we do in obedience to that word, God can be trusted not to be unjust toward those who haven't heard.

For others, however, the question betrays a discomfort with objective truth. Objective truth is that which is real and true regardless of whether we know it's real, or believe it's true. For example, the existence of God is an objective truth. God's existence doesn't hinge on our awareness of it or on our decision to believe it. He doesn't *exist* for me and *not exist* for you. Either He really exists or He doesn't: His existence does not depend on a person's acceptance of it as fact. So, if two people agree on a definition of God (a being who lives in eternal perfection in and of Himself), and one individual believes that God exists, while the other believes He does not, one is right and the other wrong. What's true for you and what's true for me are categories that simply do not apply in this discussion. The fact that there is objective truth implies that a person can at the same time be sincere, and yet assent to falsehood.

Relating all this to Jesus and salvation, John Paul II wrote about the issue, defining it as "widespread indifferentism... characterized by a religious relativism which leads to the belief that 'one religion is just as good as another'" (*The Redeemer*, 36).[24] It was in response to this phenomenon that the Catholic Church teaches:

>...the religion of Jesus, which she [the Church] proclaims through evangelization, objectively

> places man in relation with the plan of God...In
> other words, our religion effectively establishes
> with God an authentic and living relationship
> which the other religions do not succeed in
> doing... (*On Evangelization*, 53).[25]

But isn't that arrogant? Doesn't it imply that Christians are better than others? Wouldn't it contradict the part of the gospel that says God loves everyone and thereby all people are equal?

In 1982, a scare in my home city hit national news. Some people bought and took a common painkiller which had been laced with cyanide without them knowing it. As my friend Dr. Erwin Lutzer pointed out in one of his books, what they believed to be true, that this was an ordinary bottle of medicine, in this case actually wasn't.[26] As a matter of fact, their misinformation produced an effect exactly opposite of what they expected: what they thought would help them, actually killed them. The sincerity of their *faith* in those labeled bottles did not save them from the fatal consequences of a misled belief in something that wasn't objectively true. And to imply that those who didn't end up with the poisoned tablets were *better than* or *unequal* to those who did, is simply absurd.

Catholic teaching clarifies that, to say people can be misguided about truth, doesn't compromise their dignity as human beings.

> *Equality*...refers to the equal personal dignity
> of the parties in [inter-religious] dialogue, not to
> doctrinal content, nor even less to the position
> of Jesus Christ... (*Salvific Universality*, 22).[27]*

---

* The Catholic Church's teaching is aware that being in possession of truth which others do not possess can nevertheless lead to personal and communal arrogance. As a corrective, we read in the Second Vatican Council's *Dogmatic Constitution on the Church*, 14: "All the sons of the Church should remember that their exalted status is to be attributed not to their own merits but to the special grace of Christ."

If equality implies anything in the face of objective truth, it is this: everyone should have equal access to the truth—especially when it is the only truth that can save us.

> We wish to point out, above all today, that neither respect and esteem for these [other] religions nor the complexity of the questions raised is an invitation to the Church to withhold from these non-Christians the proclamation of Jesus Christ. On the contrary the Church holds that these multitudes have the right to know the riches of the mystery of Christ (Eph. 3:8)—riches in which we believe that the whole of humanity can find, in unsuspected fullness, everything that it is gropingly searching for concerning God, man and his destiny, life and death, and truth (*On Evangelization*, 53).[28]

This explains why, in the Gospel of John, sin is simply defined as unbelief in Jesus. In terms of what we have been saying, *unbelief* means not accepting the objective truth that Jesus is the Savior of the whole world. The issue staring us right in the face is this: if God is God, does He not have the right to determine how to save us? And if He loves us, as the gospel claims, can we not, and should we not, trust Him even when He offers us only one option? Today we have a major problem with anything that sounds like, "my way or the highway." But, when it comes to an all good and loving God, what may feel like *exclusivity* is, in fact, God asserting His appropriate prerogative. Indeed, Adam and Eve's sin was to respond to the serpent's proposition that *they* could become gods unto themselves: *they* could define reality; *they* could delineate "what's right for me," rather than submit to

God's sovereignty. And this rebellion is the only sin, the root of all sins. So, to refuse to accept that God has the right to and *did* determine what will save us, is to return to that original rebellion. For such a one there is no other option than to stay lost in alienation from God. And to insist on engendering a homemade sin remedy simply out of human pride, is to reach for the poisoned bottle, even after someone pleaded with us to recognize the objective truth—the contents are not what they seem.

In short, the searching modern humanity experiences about the identity and mission of Jesus of Nazareth may be expressed in more recent icons such as *Jesus Christ Superstar, The Last Temptation of Christ,* and *The Da Vinci Code*; but that searching (in some cases, even confusion) is simply not present in the Catholic Church's official teaching. The good news that Jesus, and Jesus alone, *is* the solution to our sin problem, is hailed like a clarion call for all to hear, understand, and decide upon.

> Hence, those solutions that propose a salvific action of God beyond the unique mediation of Christ would be contrary to the Christian and Catholic faith (*Salvific Universality*, 14).[29]

> "...neither is there salvation in any other" (Acts 4:12). Therefore, all must be converted to Him as He is made known by the Church's preaching (*Missionary Activity*, 7).[30]

What finally remains of the good news is the all-important biblical data on how a person receives this salvation—what "be converted" means in response to the Church's preaching.

The next chapter presents that information.

7

THE APPEAL

IN 1830, A man named George Wilson was convicted in Philadelphia for mail robbery and was sentenced to be hanged. In response to a plea from Wilson's influential friends, then-President Andrew Jackson granted the man a presidential pardon. But George Wilson, for reasons even he did not say, refused it. As can be imagined, this opened up a legal matter so involved that it escalated to the Supreme Court. There, the famous Chief Justice John Marshall handed down the decision that a pardon is but a deed on a piece of paper; its value and validity depend on acceptance by the person implicated. He commented that, indeed, it's hardly to be supposed that one under the sentence of death would refuse to accept a pardon, but if it is refused, it is no pardon. George Wilson, by his own choice, would hang. And hang he did.[1]

Thus far, our explanation of the gospel has proclaimed the great news that God has released us from sin, pardoning and justifying us once and for all by that definitive act of His Son Jesus on Calvary. God need do no more to secure what the world needs for salvation. As we have already seen in the last chapter, here in the words of John Paul II:

> The Mystery of salvation is an event which has already taken place (*Crossing*, 73–74).[2]

But a pardon offered only becomes a pardon in fact when one accepts it. What remains of the gospel is a discussion of how we *accept* God's supreme offer of grace and once and for all pardon, thus allowing it to do its work—to save us. Without this act on our part, God's salvation event is no different than what Justice Marshall said was given to George Wilson—a pardon which is but a deed on a piece of paper. Salvation will remain only an entitlement written on the pages of Scripture, without its intended effect in our lives.

Another way to get a handle on it is this. In the last chapter we read the Catholic Church's teaching that Jesus' salvation "is offered to all men as a gift of God's grace and mercy"[3] As a *gift*...from God to us, since the day of Pentecost. But, a gift given is not the same as a gift received. I can write you a check for a million dollars, but if you don't take it to the bank, my gift does not become yours. That does not change the fact that I really did give it to you; but you have not really received it and you don't enjoy its intended benefits.

God's salvation functions in exactly the same way. What has already been given to save the human race cannot be reversed. However (as the Catholic Church teaches),

> ...God is fully glorified provided that men consciously and fully accept His works of salvation, which He accomplished in Christ (*Missionary Activity*, 7).[4]

> That glory [of God the Father] consists in this: that men, knowingly, freely, and gratefully accept what God has achieved perfectly through Christ... (*Decree on the Ministry and Life of Priests*, 2).[5]

75

Consciously, fully, knowingly, freely. Head knowledge of the gospel is not adequate for salvation. For those who can think and decide for themselves, personal acceptance is necessary.

> In fact the proclamation [of the gospel] only reaches full development when it is listened to, accepted and assimilated, and when it arouses a genuine adherence in the one who has thus received it (*On Evangelization*, 23).[6]

THE TERMS OF THE NEW COVENANT

So then, what specifically constitutes personal acceptance of salvation? How does one know if he or she has received this gift?

Just as in the Old Testament, God made explicit the terms by which one was considered to be in His covenant, so, too, the New Testament and the Catholic Church's teaching specify how one enters into the new covenant of salvation. There are five internal responses which comprise the acceptance of God's gift.

One

Though we don't know why George Wilson refused the president's pardon, we do know that people could refuse such a grace—even from God—because they don't really believe themselves to be guilty. And so, the first sign of accepting salvation is to fall under personal conviction about one's sin problem.

> Awareness of our own sinfulness, including that which is inherited, is the first condition for our salvation... (*Crossing*, 58).[7]

> Conversion requires convincing of sin; it
> includes the interior judgment of conscience...
> (*On the Holy Spirit in the Life of the Church
> and the World*, 31).[8]

In other words, we begin to acknowledge what the novelist
Joseph Conrad called "some obscure and awful attribute of
our nature which, I am afraid, is not so far under the surface
as we like to think."[9] Our conscience comes into agreement
with God's diagnosis of the sin problem—down to the very
root—as outlined in the gospel. And in doing so, we give up
any shred of self-generated righteousness before God based on
our own works, merits, or religious practices.

> ...for as sinners they [all persons] stand under
> God's judgment and are incapable of turning
> by themselves to God to seek deliverance, of
> meriting their justification before God or of
> attaining salvation by their own abilities (*Joint
> Declaration*, 19).[10]

Obviously, I won't be inclined to accept God's gift of salvation if I really don't think I *need* to be saved from the problem
of sin. When the gospel is shared, many in denial about
their sin and about God's judgment of it enter a plea of Not
Guilty—or at least Not Guilty Enough to Need to Be Saved.
People don't declare bankruptcy unless they believe they have
a debt they cannot pay. Salvation only comes to those who
first accept that there's nothing on their part that can make up
for the debt owed to God because of sin. "Guilty as charged"
is an initial response of someone ready for God's redemption. As in the Twelve Step Program, a first step is to admit

that something has a power over us that is making our lives miserable. And the gospel reveals what that *something* is: an independent, rebellious nature which grieves God, alienates us from Him, and (if it hasn't already) will bring forth personal disaster. To be saved we must first come to God helpless, hopeless, desperate, broken, and lost.

Anyone who's "been there" knows this conviction is nothing casual nor is it something that remains in the head alone. A person who hears the gospel and glibly responds, "Yeah, I know I'm a sinner," has not entered into the conviction of which we speak. To respond to the gospel, one must allow the Holy Spirit to prick the heart with the weight, offense, sadness, and harm of one's own sin inclination. Here we allow ourselves to see our sin burden as God in His purity and perfect holiness sees it, not as we would prefer to see it. Here we enter the experience of those who were the first to hear the message of salvation on Pentecost. Acts 2:37 tells us that they were "cut to the heart." The Catholic spiritual writer Fr. Thomas Merton described this reality as nothing less than "dread."* The *Catechism of the Catholic Church* also affirms that,

---

* "It, [dread] is the deep...awareness of a *basic antagonism between the self and God* due to estrangement from him by perverse attachment to a 'self' which is mysterious and illusory. Nor is this estrangement purely and simply a matter to be adjusted juridically...by the reception of sacraments with minimal good dispositions...This will not liberate one from 'dread' and 'night' as long as he tends to cling to the empty illusion of a separate self, inclined to resist God...Even without acts of sin, we have in ourselves an *inclination* to sin and rebellion, an inclination to falsity and to evasion. "It is natural for one in this case to dread the loss of his faith...and cling desperately to whatever will seem to preserve the last shreds of belief. So he struggles, sometimes frantically, to recover a sense of comfort and conviction in formulated truths or familiar religious practices...But the more he struggles, the less comfort and assurance he has, and the more powerless he sees himself to be. "Now we can understand that the full maturity of the spiritual life cannot be reached unless we first pass through the dread, anguish, trouble and fear that necessarily accompany the inner crisis of 'spiritual death' in which we finally abandon attachment to our exterior self and surrender completely to Christ."(Thomas Merton, *Contemplative Prayer* (Garden City, NY: Image Books, 1971), 97–99, 110.) Likewise, at my last retreat before entering the Order of Friars Minor, I'll never forget hearing a Franciscan priest preach, "Nothing happens in the spiritual life until one is 'cut to the heart.'"

> This conversion of heart is accompanied by a
> salutary pain and sadness which the Fathers
> called *animi cruciatus* (affliction of spirit)...[11]

This is actually a primal move of the Holy Spirit in the hearts of those who open themselves to the gospel.

> But to do its work grace must uncover sin so as
> to convert our hearts and bestow on us "righ-
> teousness to eternal life through Jesus Christ
> our Lord (Rom. 5:21)." Like a physician who
> probes the wound before treating it, God, by
> his Word and by his Spirit, casts a living light
> on sin... (*Catechism*, 1848).[12]

There comes a point when people going down in quicksand face the crisis that either they will be rescued or they will perish. By nature, all humans are already sinking in the quicksand of sin. To recognize this fact about one's self, and to enter fully (head *and* heart) into the crisis, is a prerequisite position for accepting God's plan to save—indeed, His plan for *anything* in our lives. Here we join the apostle Paul, whose words about his own sin condition powerfully express that of us all: "What a wretched man I am! Who will *rescue* me from this body doomed to death?" (Rom. 7:24, emphasis added). Not, "Who will help me?" The word *rescue* is a synonym for *save*. There is something transformative that happens to a person who experiences this crisis.

Two

Once my head agrees with and my heart is cut into by the reality of my sin as God sees it, I must pick up the responsibility and decide what I want to do with it. You see, God has always laid down an escape route from any sin. If free will moved us into sin, God in His love will give us the grace for another free-will choice to move out of it. The biblical word for this choice is *repentance*. Repentance is not just saying, "I'm sorry." It is an act of sorrowfully renouncing the sin and making an honest decision of the will to turn away from it in the future.

But the repentance the gospel proposes is quite distinct. You see, repentance and forgiveness of sins were nothing new to the people of the Old Testament. The temple sacrifices even offered a system whereby transgressions were assuredly pardoned by God. The only problem was, even this God-ordained method could never fix the root issues that produced these sins in the first place. Confess as they might, the Jews were still stuck with the reality that they were sinners by nature, with no hope of ultimate reconciliation with God.

The New Covenant offers something more than what people already had in the Old Testament. As we've already seen, Jesus can make sinners right with God by His own merits, overpower that root rebellion in us, and recreate our hearts with new, divine life. And so, if repentance is *always* the way for sinners to be reconciled with God, and if Jesus offers reconciliation at a place that was not possible in the old covenant (at the bottom-line issue of our rebellion itself), the gospel must call for a repentance at this new level. Thus the plan of salvation requires a radical, complete turning away, not only from the *symptoms* of rebellion, but from *being* rebellious. It is not so much a repentance for what I've *done*, but for what's in my nature that produces it—a heart that keeps asserting its own way before God. In other words, I repent not of my sins, but of the sin *inclination* in me.

If I am under conviction about sin, willingness to repent then amounts to nothing less than making a decision to reorient my whole life, once and for all. The biblical word for this type of repentance is *conversion*, a translation of the Greek term *metanoia*, which means a new change of mindset about all of life. This was exactly what the prodigal son experienced when he "came to his senses" (Luke 15:17) and decided to return home and do things his dad's way. Catholic moral theologians call it "the fundamental option": a foundational decision about how one wants to live life in relation to God, a decision made in the heart "where the person *decides for or against God* (cf. Jer. 31:33; Deut. 6:5; 29:3; Isa. 29:13; Ezek. 36:26; Matt. 6:21; Luke 8:15; Rom. 5:5)" (emphasis added, *Catechism*, 368).[13]

Two further notes are in order. First, I've seen people avoid this conversion because they fear they won't be able to live out their intention. But an act of will to turn from the dominion of sin says nothing about our power to carry out that resolve, and one who has entered into the previous response, we explained, has already settled that issue. There we openly admit we *are* powerless to kick the sin habit. It will *have* to take divine power to make us live according to our decision. And, thanks be to God, that's exactly what the good news promises He will give us if we are honestly repentant.

Secondly, if by definition repentance means an honest decision to renounce what displeases God and turn away from it in the future, and if in *this* type of repentance we are turning from sin itself toward a whole new life, we can see how one must enter this conversion with a once and for all mentality. The new covenant, like any covenant, is a choice that is only meant to be made once, with the intention of allowing it to define one's whole covenanted future. Like all other such choices (marriage, circumcision, etc.), one may struggle with maintaining the covenanted relationship, but a covenant once made remains an unrepeatable reference point for the entire duration, a fundamental option. Couples do not remarry every time they resolve a marriage difficulty; as a matter of fact, they often appeal to their till death do us part decision as the very source of strength and grace they need when that covenant is challenged. This dynamic represents the vital difference between the repentance of the Old Testament—even the practice of those who "go to confession" to be forgiven—and the conversion choice to accept new covenant salvation for all eternity.

To summarize:

> Interior repentance is a radical reorientation of our whole life, a return, a conversion to God with all our heart, an end of sin, a turning away from evil, with repugnance toward the evil actions we have committed (*Catechism*, 1431).[14]

And as St. Augustine said,

> They aren't really choosing a new life, after all, unless they are sorry for the old one.[15]

Three

Desperately, hopelessly, helplessly lost sinners who repent of sin can be saved if they also believe the good news that what Jesus did on the cross is *enough* to save. In the first two responses, we admit that we have a terminal illness—sin—and we cry out that we're ready to be healed from it. In this response we believe that God's antidote will work, and we stop seeking a second opinion. Having examined the gospel's claims about the death and resurrection of Jesus, we move beyond an "I hope so" response, and really decide that His completed work *can* produce in our lives what the gospel says it will. As in the second step of the Twelve Step Program, we "come to believe" that this higher power can restore us. This is what's meant by faith, as it applies to salvation. John Paul II articulated the need for this faith as he wrote,

> Everyone who looks for salvation, not only the Christian, must stop before the Cross of Christ. Will he be willing to accept the truth of the Paschal Mystery or not? Will he have faith? This is yet another issue (*Crossing*, 73).[16]

Four

Once the convicted sinner has been moved to that about-face repentance and also believes the good news that God can and will save him or her through the finished work of Calvary, it is time to step into that new, saving relationship. One must decide to transfer one's trust to Jesus alone as Savior, once and for all. Here we "put all our eggs in one basket," and rely on Christ alone.

Again, as always, we're talking about more than head knowledge here. There's a big difference between saying, "I've always believed that Jesus is the Savior," and "Jesus is *my* Savior." Likewise, if I am willing to accept Him in this position of my life, it only stands to reason that I must take my trust out of everything else I was relying on to make me right with God. In other words, if I were to die tonight, appear before God for judgment, and He were to ask me, "Why should I let you into my Kingdom?" I would have spiritually torn up the list of reasons I used to have ready for that moment and replaced it with but one appeal: "I trust the blood of Jesus as my redemption." This the Evangelical brethren capture in the celebrated phrase, "through Christ alone." The Catholic Church affirms the truth of that phrase in the *Joint Declaration on the Doctrine of Justification* with Lutherans, as together we say,

> Through Christ alone are we justified, when we receive this salvation in faith.[17]

If this is how I desire to be justified, then, as in any covenant, I will want to go to Jesus and tell Him my intention to "make the switch" for all eternity.

So, credal profession is not what constitutes receiving salvation. On the part of those who have the faculty of reason, a conscious decision to abandon all other means and to transfer one's trust to Jesus once and for all, is necessary. As John Paul II wrote,

> Conversion means accepting by a personal decision the saving sovereignty of Christ and becoming his disciple (*The Mission*, 46).[18]

Five

One internal response remains: each person must make a covenant decision to surrender his or her life to Jesus once and for all. This submission is but the logical reversal of our rebellion and independence which we forsook in the repentance response. It is a decision which must positively replace the negative state of sin of which we were convicted:

> The "obedience of faith" (Rom. 16:26; cf. 1:5...) must be given to God who reveals, an obedience by which man entrusts his whole self freely

to God, offering the full submission of intellect and will to God who reveals… (*Dogmatic Constitution on Divine Revelation*, 5)[19]

This is what is meant by a profession of Jesus as *Lord*. And, as we said above about His role as Savior, mere credal profession does not suffice for salvation. An illustration will help. When a loved one dies, especially if suddenly or tragically, people are often heard saying, "I just can't believe it!" Even as they view the body at the wake, it's not uncommon to hear, "I see him right there in front of me, but it's just so hard to believe." What is being articulated is that the mind certainly can perceive and know the truth that the person is gone; but it is difficult to accept the *implications* of this truth, for if one *surrenders* to the fact, life will change drastically. So it is with the lordship of Jesus. Anyone can profess, "Oh, I know Jesus is Lord. I've always believed that." But it's quite a different affair to live with the *implications* of that truth for one's own life if one were to *surrender* to it. If I surrender to His lordship, if I really give Him permission to control my life, things *will* begin to change drastically.

So, head faith and surrender are two different realities. The gospel is not interested in the first (for even the powers of darkness believe that Jesus is Lord); it calls for the second—a free-will decision to put one's life under the control of Jesus from here on in. As Fr. Raniero Cantalamessa, preacher to the Pope's household, once spoke,

> To say, "Jesus is Lord" means, in fact, to make a decision. It is as though saying: Jesus Christ is "my" Lord…[20]

Primary Conversion

So, these are the five internal responses to the message of salvation which verify that one has truly accepted God's gift. This is what Evangelicals mean when they talk of "accepting Jesus Christ as personal Lord and Savior." Now, these words can cause some to bristle, admittedly. Many in my Church write them off as something positively un-Catholic. Some of the more educated would be quick to point out that "accepting Jesus Christ as personal Lord and Savior" isn't even found in what Evangelicals claim is their sourcebook, the Bible. And they are correct. But neither is the word *Trinity* found in the Bible. New words or phrases can be created by post-New Testament Christians to explain biblical realities validly. What we have demonstrated in this chapter is that *personal acceptance* is a non-negotiable aspect of salvation, and it is internally consistent with both biblical revelation *and* Catholic teaching. As this citation from Paul VI's *On Evangelization in the Modern World* summarizes,

> ...each individual gains them [the Kingdom of God and salvation] through a total interior renewal which the Gospel calls *metanoia*; it is a radical conversion, a profound change of mind and heart.[21]

When these "terms of the new covenant" are entered into, when a person has in fact been converted as we have described, he or she *knows* internally that God's gift has been received. How? The Holy Spirit begins to break forth in an unprecedented way within the sphere of that person's life, and he or she experiences it. Then (and both Catholics and Evangelicals agree on this much) baptism is the external sign of the conversion reality.

> Always, Baptism is seen as connected with faith: "Believe in the Lord Jesus, and you will be saved..." (*Catechism*, 1226).[22]

We will have more to say on how this relates specifically to Catholics later. The point here is that the *inner* reality constitutes an essential component of accepting salvation from God.

> This conversion, to be sure, must be regarded as a beginning. Yet it is sufficient that a man realize that he has been snatched away from sin and led into the mystery of the love of God, who has called him to enter into a personal relationship with him in Christ (*Missionary Activity*, 13).[23]

One more important point before moving on: I've heard Catholics respond to this message by saying, "Well, I agree there has to be conversion. But conversion is a *process*, not a one-time event." There are two problems with this response. First, let's say you met a couple who introduced themselves as Joe and Mary Smith. Then, in the course of conversation, you asked, "When were you married?" and they answered, "Marriage is a process: we don't believe it's necessary to 'get married.'" You might have some legitimate questions about exactly what kind of relationship they have. It is the nature of any covenant that there be an alpha-point at which the involved parties enter into the terms of the covenant. If we accept the proposition that marriage is, indeed, a covenant, we will also conclude that Mary and Joe may think they're married, but may not be. Likewise if you were to ask me, "When were you born?" and I replied, "I'm born anew every day...life is a process," you might be tempted to say, "Cut the philosophizing and just answer the question!" Gestation is a process. Growth is a process. But birth is a relatively definable moment that separates the two. So also with our birth into the new life. There is a point at which a person who is capable of making a decision, must "cross the line" into the new covenant, a time when he or she exits the "birth canal" and transitions from sinner to justified, slave of sin to freed from sin, old life to new life.

The second problem is that Catholics who respond this way have not read their Church documents. The Catholic Church not only affirms the need for this conversion (as we have seen in this chapter), but even creates its own term for it: "the first and fundamental conversion" (*Catechism*, 1427).[24] And this is how it is described:

> It is by faith in the Gospel and by Baptism (cf.
> Acts 2:38) that one renounces evil and gains
> salvation, that is, the forgiveness of all sins and
> the gift of new life (*Catechism*, 1427).[25*]

Catholics and Evangelicals alike believe that they will still contend with the flesh in some way after conversion. But the whole picture has been reframed because the root problem has been dealt with. The Christian life, like any covenant, then becomes a matter of living out on a daily basis the dynamic one entered into once and for all—repentance, faith, trust, surrender—but with

---

* Some Evangelicals may disagree with Catholic teaching on the role of baptism in salvation. The point here is one I've made already: the Catholic Church teaches that (however one views baptism) the sacramental action does not represent an isolated reality: for those who have the use of reason, the "first and fundamental conversion" is necessary to receive salvation. More about how Catholic teaching views the relationship between the two will follow in chapter nine.

the power of the indwelling Holy Spirit.* *That* is a process. But every process must begin with a starting point; every salvation must begin with a "first and fundamental conversion."

There's simply no replacement for it once one has heard the gospel. All attempts to circumvent or dial down this conversion are but conscious or unconscious efforts to maintain control and independence rather than surrender to the loving "Hound of Heaven." Not even being an official Church leader can substitute for this conversion. I am often heard telling Catholics, "Ordination does not equal salvation." Yes, even a priest needs to be saved. Let me tell you how it happened to me.

---

* This ongoing return to one's new covenant intentions is what the *Catechism of the Catholic Church* calls "second conversion," a reality which is "uninterrupted," and is "the movement of a 'contrite heart,' drawn and moved by grace" (1428). This also embodies Luther's notion "simul justus et peccator" (at the same time righteous and sinner): he correctly perceived that one who is saved still needs to deal with the old flesh which sets itself in enmity with the new spirit (cf. Gal. 5:17). The *Joint Declaration on the Doctrine of Justification* articulates the agreement of Lutherans and Catholics on this issue: "But the justified must all through constantly look to God's unconditional justifying grace. They also are continuously exposed to the power of sin still pressing its attacks (cf. Rom. 6:12–14) and are not exempt from a lifelong struggle against the contradiction to God within the selfish desires of the old Adam (cf. Gal. 5:16; Rom. 7:7–10). The justified must also ask God daily for forgiveness as in the Lord's Prayer (Matt. 6:12; 1 John 1:9), and are ever again called to conversion and penance, and are ever again granted forgiveness." (28) "Together we hear the exhortation, 'Therefore do not let sin exercise dominion in your mortal bodies, to make you obey their passions' (Rom. 6:12). To this extent, Lutherans and Catholics together understand the Christian as *simul justus et peccator*…" (Annex to the Official Common Statement, 2A).

8

THE REALITY OF THE GOSPEL

YES, THE GOSPEL is real. I know so for myself.
Being raised in church, I was always a spiritual
person with an openness to God. But I would be less
than honest if I didn't also say that, early on, I knew that I
needed God. You see, due to a lot of family pain, I became the
proverbial "poster boy" for what was often taught later on in
the 60s: "we all have a big love-shaped hole inside of us." That
was certainly true in my case, and I was well aware of it at a
young age. So, because Christian religion was a normal part
of upbringing in my little world, it was very easy to seek sol-
ace and love in this divine being, who fascinated me anyway.

But upon reaching adolescence, with everything else I was
outgrowing, my childish and sometimes superstitious connection
to God began to change. I embarked on the questioning search
normal for that period of life, and even God Himself was put in
the docket. I simply had to find out whether all this stuff I was
taught about Him was really true, or not. Did God *really* exist, or
is He some kind of psychological crutch we made up to help us
get by? If He is for real, how come I do not see the things I read
and hear about in the Bible happening today? I wasn't cynical
about my confusion, for I couldn't deny that every once in awhile
I did have a spiritual experience at church. Yet, those experiences

seemed so disconnected from the rest of my reality. In short, I wanted to believe, but didn't know how it could all fit together.

Then something happened which shifted my gears and catapulted me into a new phase of my life story. Right before Christmas break in my junior year of high school, we had an all-school Mass at which two priest religion teachers preached the homily together. Both were men that I knew, highly respected, and viewed as role models. Their content and delivery made such an impact on me, and on the entire student body, that during the next two days at school there was a tangible spiritual energy in the air I had never experienced before. In the halls, between classes, being together, it seemed that God had come for a visit to Quigley South. And, for me, that meant He had transcended the church building, and showed up in my real life. Just what I was waiting for!

And I never forgot it. It put a hunger in me to know Him more. The retreats and student council training I attended from May of my junior year on, included further events confirming that Jesus could be tangible when people share themselves in a real way with one another. But each event proved to be a *high* which only lasted awhile. And I wanted more.

Finally, at the end of my senior year, two things transpired that set me on the course of my destiny of salvation. First, in the final trimester, I took an evening seminar religion class simply entitled, "Jesus." As part of the class, we were required to read the entire Gospel of Mark. This, in effect, reintroduced me to the Bible, for I had never read it in this way, nor read it as a person seeking to sort things out for himself. The seminar was fascinating, and it unexpectedly fed my desire to know the Lord. What's more, in the class, I saw my peers discussing and taking the Bible seriously. That seemed to legitimate this spiritual search I was on.

All in all, the course opened a desire in me to discover more of the Lord as revealed in the Bible, and to stay close to the Bible in my spiritual quest.

Secondly, since my high school years occurred in the post-60s era, its hippie, *far-out* culture naturally affected our institution, full of young people as it was. One of the effects was that in my senior year, some schoolmates were becoming what we called "Jesus freaks." Guys I knew and respected were now wearing crosses *on the outside*, toting Bibles, and talking openly about Jesus. At the time it was not as culturally offensive as it might seem today. In that era, everyone was out there with their stuff, advertising openly what they were *into*. It just so happened these guys were into Jesus. And I admired them. In a sense, I wanted what they had. So I accepted an invitation to attend an after-school Bible study led by one of their friends who was allowed to come in from the outside. Somehow in the exchange, I heard the words, "Jesus loves you." Now of course, I already knew that, in the head. But I seemed to hear it for the first time in my heart. *In my heart.* And it was a proposition I didn't want to let go of.

You see, I certainly knew enough facts about the Lord—He's almighty, He's holy, He's eternal, etc. But in my heart there still was a *disconnect*. Part of the jumble inside was a notion that, because God was the perfect, all-knowing being, He ultimately didn't want to have a lot to do with the likes of me. Yes, every once in a while I would experience His presence, but even at those times I could also feel the weight of my sin, which often made me feel like running away in shame. But when the Bible teacher suggested that the Lord loves us *no matter what*, something got connected inside.

It even helped make sense of the sometimes doubt I had about God's very existence. If, by definition, God is the highest and greatest being that is, wouldn't it make sense that He would be defined by the highest reality we know—love? Doesn't the Bible even say, "God *is* love"? (1 John 4:16, emphasis added). Could it be that many like me who struggled with the belief in God's existence simply hadn't come to terms with who God really is? I quickly reached a conclusion: if you're going to believe in a God at all, He *must* be defined as love.

So, for the next few months (and this was how I learned to pray), I would sit quietly in my room at night, and proclaim that good news to myself over and over. "God loves me. God *loves* me! *God* loves me! God loves *me*!" At times I found it easy to believe it, at times I didn't. At times I would argue with God, giving Him the whole list of reasons why He shouldn't love me. (Remember, I was well aware of the many ways I did not please Him.) But, whenever I would argue, He would bring me right back to the statement on which I was meditating and say, "That's the *truth*, no matter what your head or emotions tell you. Believe the good news."

As I did, I felt like I was beginning to find what I longed for my whole life—love from the only person whose opinion and judgment ultimately mattered, from the One who *knows everything there is to know about me and still decides to say,* "I love you." Years later I ran across a title by the Jesuit psychologist, Fr. John Powell, *If You Really Knew Me, Would You Still Love Me?* I believe this is a question which, consciously or unconsciously, haunts everyone on the planet. But the good news I discovered was that there is One who *does really* know me—sins and all; yet He answers that jarring question with a resounding "Yes!" His is the unconditional love I—and the whole world—was searching for. And *I found it*!

It seemed, also, that He didn't want me to lose it. Over and over and over, in the secret place of my heart, the Lord just kept loving me—even when I couldn't seem to love myself. As a result, something new began to be released in me. I started to experience an internal peace I had not known. I also felt His real acceptance; and this especially turned out to be a vital anchor because, during that time, my relationship with my parents grew particularly stormy. In the midst of it all, though, I had a quiet joy fostered by a very real personal relationship with my divine Father—a relationship *no one* could take away from me.

ONLY THE BEGINNING

But this was not yet salvation. It was a discovery of the Lord's unconditional love as the basis of the rest of my relationship with Him. From there I spent three years reading Scripture and practicing the discipline of prayer in order to build that personal relationship. Good liturgy and preaching continued to be a vital source of connection with Him in a communal setting.

But don't get me wrong. I also continued enjoying my sin. I was very headstrong, prideful, and in control. Bitterness and unforgiveness determined too many of my relationships. Having done well academically, I also relied on my own intelligence a lot. My root problem of rebellion and independence also expressed itself in what St. Paul said as he described sin in Ephesians 2:3—being "ruled entirely by...our own ideas." So there was a battle brewing between my growing spiritual self and the rest of me that was marked with sin.

In attending Christian gatherings, I began to hear more and more talk of accepting Jesus as your personal Lord and Savior. Well, it wasn't hard to see that He wasn't really Lord of my life.

But I kept that issue stowed in my head, safely hidden behind all my correct theology, where I didn't really have to deal with it.

Until one evening when I was in chapel, thanking the Lord for His love that had been *so* unconditional over these years, especially in light of my obvious sinfulness. I had been drawn to pray right after the first TV showing of Franco Zeffirreli's movie, *Jesus of Nazareth*. Being a visual person, the movie impacted me as one of those "you were there" moments, and it drew me to want to love and follow Jesus more than ever. But, as I was praying, I heard the Lord speak directly to my heart: "You're thanking Me for giving Myself completely to you; now I want you to give yourself completely to Me. *I want you to accept Me as your personal Lord and Savior.*" I certainly knew what He was asking—that my future, my purpose, and my destiny from that point on, be nothing less than to serve and live for Him. He wanted my surrender.

It's important to know that at this time, I wasn't 100 percent sure about the calling to the priesthood—which made the Lord's word an even greater challenge. You see, one way or another, *I* would be taking charge of the plans for my life. And the options were many. In college I had been successful at theater and the roar of the greasepaint still buzzed in my ears. With higher training, I could have also entered a career in teaching, vocal musical performance, or social activism. But, here was Jesus saying that He wanted to own me—which meant that my ego-centered plans had to crash. I might still end up doing any of those activities, He said, but *He* would make the decision, and they would be enslaved to the Kingdom, not to my own purposes. "Seek ye first..." (Matt. 6:33). So, after seriously pondering this choice and what I knew it would cost me, I spoke to Him these exact words: "OK, Lord, you got me."

But, that still wasn't salvation. One of the reasons I know is that my life really didn't change much after that night. I was sincere in my decision, but I was to learn that I couldn't fulfill it until some other issues were confronted. Yes, I considered myself a disciple who had now left my nets at the seashore; I even joined the Franciscan Order as an expression of this. My future was surrendered and I was, indeed, committed to follow Jesus. But (did you notice?) I had not yet faced the pivotal issue of the new covenant—the issue which has prevented every disciple from Peter to the present from fulfilling the desire to serve Jesus Christ; my sin problem remained unaddressed.

About a year and a half later, I had another prayer experience. This time I was expressing to the Lord my frustration at how inconsistent our relationship seemed. I would literally feel Him right there on one day—even had miraculous physical healings through prayer—but the next day He'd seem a million miles away. "Lord, what gives?" I asked. After showing me that the problem was not on His end (it never is), He convinced me I was still missing the new life which the Holy Spirit brings. So, naturally, that's what I probed into during this prayer. And right then and there, He sovereignly taught me about the Person and baptism of the Holy Spirit. I knew I had a relationship with the Father and the Son, but not a personal relationship with Holy Spirit; and previous to this, I never understood the baptism of the Spirit, even though I had heard of the term. So finally, I asked the Holy Spirit to introduce Himself to me...and He did! A physical wave of His presence entered me, starting at the heels of my feet and proceeding to the crown of my head. And that "took me around the corner" as far as salvation is concerned.

For, one of the first things the Holy Spirit did was to fill in the blanks of what was missing in my acceptance of the gospel.

He began to show me my sin. Then He led me to the full message we have presented here, until I repented once and for all and entrusted my sin burden to Jesus alone, believing that His completed work at Calvary would save me. My "first and fundamental conversion" was now complete.

And the effects? First of all, there's nothing like believing, as 1 Peter 2:21 attests, Jesus suffered for *my* sake. For *my* sake! When I ponder all He actually went through out of sheer love, just so *I* could have all that's included in salvation, I am filled with gratitude, awe, and love beyond description. Receiving His act of salvation has raised my personal relationship with Him to a new level: for, truly "No one has greater love than this, to lay down one's life for one's friends" (John 15:13, NAB), and now I revel in this love.

Then, to believe that He rose from the dead, not only as His own victory, but precisely to give *me* this victory—to experience that I am now included in His triumph and that the Enemy's rancid darkness no longer possesses the power it once had over me—this brings a joy and hope I had never known in my previous struggles. It positions me at a new starting point—one in which the sting of my sins is already removed; one in which right conduct now becomes a matter of not my ability but of His ability in me. Yes, I must continue to cooperate and stay repentant at the cross, but I now bear a yoke which "is easy" and a burden "light" (Matt. 11:30).

There is also no substitute for the belief that God has forgiven me once and for all, that I am made right before Him, and that I am heaven-bound (cf. Rom. 5:1–2.) Repentance is no longer a matter of redredging all the shame and pain that covered me before I was converted, nor of wondering, "Will He forgive me for *this* one?" If I truly renew my salvation repentance, oh, the joy that returns when He renews His forgiveness! And through it all there's no greater consolation than to know that, because I accepted Jesus' righteousness (cf. Phil. 3:9), it's OK not to be perfect yet (cf. Phil. 3:12).

There's also no greater thrill than to live in an "Acts of the Apostles reality." I have witnessed times when the Holy Spirit flows through our hands and we see the sick recover, when we pray for and call forth miracles and they happen, or when we exercise supernatural gifts in ministry which we recognize come only from Him (cf. 1 Cor. 12:8–11). There are times of individual or corporate worship in which the presence of God is so tangibly marvelous that we taste a bit of heaven. Yet, these are but manifestations of the greatest Acts of the Apostles reality: the fact that those who are saved are now in possession of nothing less than eternal life. Can it get any better than that?

All in all, I am so glad to be on this side of the line of salvation. I can honestly say I've found what my heart was looking for (and what sin promised, but couldn't deliver). I found out that the love-shaped hole inside of me is really a *God*-shaped hole, which only He can fill. And the reason I do what I do with my life is that I see *everyone*, in some way or another, looking for what I found: unconditional love, inner peace, and joy. The good news I learned is that it's all there waiting for us through salvation in Jesus Christ, which only God can give and which we don't have to allow anyone to take away.

EASY STREET?

Don't get me wrong. I'm not implying that salvation instantly transfers one to cloud nine. Jesus himself promised a cross to His followers, and He said if we bypass it, we really don't belong to Him. My life also testifies to the fact that when you are saved, you don't spend a lot of time on Easy Street.

For example, almost immediately when I was led to conversion by the Holy Spirit, I began to feel a *disconnect* with those around me who did not have a testimony of salvation. Some thought I was weird; others rejected this new aspect of my life. Especially, as a Catholic, I struggled with being myself when it meant I would have to be a "fool for Christ." Ultimately, I lost some close friends, while other relationships grew distant for lack of sharing that old common ground. This was part of the price I paid, and it was painful.

After conversion, the Spirit really began to operate on me. And I do mean *operate*. He began to show me that so much of the sin in my life that needed to go was a result of the inner pain I experienced growing up. And that pain would need to be healed through intensive inner surgery before the sin could disappear. That information alone came at a price: His spiritually probing scalpel hurt. He also showed me how sin had clustered in addictions in my life. I had a sweet tooth that wouldn't quit (got chocolate?), and my family background left me with a tendency to become dependent on unhealthy relationships. After awhile it was obvious that I needed extra help to deal with these struggles, and eventually He led me to Christian counseling and inner healing ministries.

In one sense these were the darkest years of my life. But through tears, anger, and confusion, the Lord stood patiently by my side, releasing real healing and deliverance upon me. There were hours when it felt like the only one I had to hang onto was Him, but He got me through. Eventually I learned how to receive ministry from ordinary members of Christ's Body as well. Big chunks of my heart were released from the pain of rejection, abandonment, and hatred. In its place I learned how to respect and love myself, while also forgiving, reconciling, or moving on in relationships.

So my new life has indeed been *new*, but it has been anything but pain free. Yet, I've learned that dealing with the pain of life (which by nature we'd rather avoid) becomes an opportunity for Jesus to display His victory. All in all, I have found no better way of living than in a saving, personal relationship with Him. With the apostle Paul I can honestly and joyfully say, "I believe *nothing* can happen that will outweigh the supreme advantage of knowing Christ Jesus my Lord" (Phil. 3:8, emphasis added).

9

THE RE-EVANGELIZATION

BILLY GRAHAM REPORTED that in the 1980s he attended a reception in Osaka, Japan, at which the governor of Osaka gave an address. At one point in the speech, the official turned to him and said, "Dr. Graham, why is it that the Church in Japan is still only 1 percent, which is about the same as it was in the seventeenth century? I believe it is because the gospel has not been made clear to the Japanese people. I hope that you will make it clear."[1]

The previous chapters have demonstrated that the Catholic Church presents a plethora of teaching from varied sources, affirming the truths of the *kerygma*. But our presentation would not be complete without addressing a glaring issue: if the gospel is true, Catholics are in massive need of evangelization. Unlike the situation in Japan, Catholics in this country *do* attend church; but years and years of experience tell me that, *like* in Japan, a disquietingly low number have had the gospel made clear to them, leaving a dramatic need for someone to do exactly that.* And—the Catholic Church has another wealth of statements which confirm these observations.

We start with what I consider to be the charter of my own ministry. In the very guts of Paul VI's document which we've quoted widely, *On Evangelization in the Modern World*, we

---

* *Without exception*, every time I preach the salvation message to a Catholic audience, there are people who ask, "How come I've never heard this before?"

read something which takes the temperature of Catholics in relation to the gospel. I've already quoted some of it, but what it says in its entirety is startling:

> The first proclamation is addressed especially to those who have never heard the Good News of Jesus, or to children. But, as a result of the frequent situations of dechristianization in our day, it proves equally necessary for innumerable people who have been baptized but who live quite outside Christian life, for simple people who have a certain faith but an imperfect knowledge of the foundations of that faith, for intellectuals who need to know Jesus Christ in a light different from the instruction they received as a child, and for many others.[2]

Please don't overlook a word of this meaty statement. Let me break it down into its component parts.

- There are forces today which dechristianize—try to alter what Christianity is really all about.

- Therefore it is possible for one to be baptized in a church context which still enables him or her to live "quite outside" the Christian life. The water of baptism alone does not guarantee the change of life Christianity offers.

- People who fit this category need the first proclamation. It is *necessary*. Why? Because only the information provided by the first proclamation leads to the conversion necessary for our salvation once we reach an age at which we can understanding its requirements.

- "Innumerable people" fit this category. *Webster's* defines the word *innumerable* as "too many to be counted."

- There are also "simple people who have a certain faith." These are the Catholics who sincerely believe in God, faithfully go to church, but have not entered the first and fundamental conversion because practicing their religion is all they've been shown. The first proclamation is also *necessary* for them because without it, their notion of being a good Catholic will not save.

- There are Catholic adults who seriously seek answers to questions that were never answered for them as children. Only the gospel can resolve their ultimate spiritual issues, so it is *necessary* for them as well.

- There are *many others* for whom the salvation message is *necessary.*

- This message is *equally* necessary for all these Catholics—as *necessary* as for those listed who have never heard it before.

And here's the amazing implication you don't want to miss: the leadership of the Catholic Church is under no pretence that people who call themselves Catholics—even practicing Catholics—have heard, understood, and responded to the salvation message we profess in our official teaching. That assertion, to coin a contemporary phrase, is *huge!*

As a matter of fact, this claim was not entirely new to the publishing of *On Evangelization in the Modern World*. Five years previous, for example, Archbishop Patricio Flores (then an assistant bishop) in San Antonio, Texas, offered the same thoughts as he reflected on his local Church situation. *The Texas Catholic* newspaper had this report:

> ..."They [many] took the position that there was no need to worry about the faith of the Mexicans because of their love for the blessed Virgin. We cannot," he continued, "expect miracles to cover up our stupidity. The Indians, from whom we are descended," the bishop said, "were never really evangelized, they were sacralized. They love Mary and the sacraments but never learned to love Jesus or His gospel." Unfortunately, Bishop Flores pointed out, the same situation exists today in many places. "Many priests still don't preach the gospel to their Mexican-American parishioners..."[3]

Nor has this issue resolved itself since *On Evangelization in the Modern World* came out in 1975. A few years later, John Paul II reiterated the problem, in a document about the need for solid teaching within Catholic Christianity. Here he distinguished "the initial conversion-bringing proclamation of the gospel" from catechesis (teaching) which follows for the purpose of maturing that initial faith. Applying this paradigm to his contemporary Church situation, however, he added,

> But in catechetical practice, this model order must allow for the fact that the initial evange-

lization has often not taken place (*Catechesis*, 19).[4]

Experience has continued to bear out what these Catholic leaders have prophetically taught. Recently, the Barna Group (a Christian version of the Gallup poll) took a nationwide survey of responses to this statement: If a person is generally good, or does enough good things for others during their life, they will earn a place in heaven. Of the Catholic respondents, only 8 percent disagreed strongly; including these, only 16 percent disagreed at all. Meanwhile, a whopping 79 percent agreed with the statement, with 54 percent of them saying they agreed *strongly*![5] Conclusion: the vast majority of Catholics is either not sure about the basis of their salvation or erroneously trust in their own righteousness. And, that's more than thirty years after our key text above from *On Evangelization in the Modern World* was written!

Also, a member of my ministry recently embarked on an innovative way of evangelizing. Being an extroverted person, she finds it easy to converse individually with people she meets out in the public. If it seems appropriate to the conversation, she asks if the person would like to participate in a survey she's doing. If the person responds positively, she says, "We are told in the Bible, 'Repent and believe the good news.' Now, to *repent* means to turn away from sin and renounce it. But what is 'the good news'?" This question then usually leads into an evangelistic conversation. She also posed the same question to a group of youth being prepared for confirmation at a Catholic school in which she was subbing. Using this approach, she has interviewed seventy people in all at the time of this writing. Of the seventy, forty-two were Catholic (eighteen youth and twenty-four adults).

Obviously, her findings are not as professionally fine-tuned as the Barna survey or a Gallup poll, but I believe they are still worth reporting. Of the seventy people, three non-Catholic Christians could articulate the basics of the salvation message when asked. The Catholics could give bits and pieces of the good news, but never spoke about how one actually receives salvation. No Catholic mentioned the Church's official teachings. In the evangelistic conversations, when she posed the further question, "Well, what about Jesus? Why did He die on the cross?" the Catholics who correctly answered that He died for our sins, still said (in so many words), "But down here I'm still trying to win this battle," without being able to put the two realities together. Their knowledge about Jesus was more like something floating in the head somewhere which they couldn't see functionally related to the rest of their lives.[*]

Conclusion: Catholics are no different than the majority of the population—they have an unclear notion of salvation, and little knowledge of the salvation message.

I must say, this research simply confirms my own perceptions after evangelizing in the Catholic context since 1986. Experience seems to corroborate our Church's teaching that the "essential content" of the gospel has been "modified" (*On Evangelization*, 25)[6] and "dechristianized" (*On Evangelization*, 52)[7] to the extent that Catholics need to *hear* it anew, so they may *understand* and *respond* to it if they so choose. This is what led John Paul II (as late as 1990) to issue a striking call for the "re-evangelization" of Catholics:

> There is an intermediate situation, particularly
> in countries with ancient Catholic roots, and
> occasionally in the younger churches as well,

---

[*]   Interview with Arlene Paolicchi, November 18, 2009.

where entire groups of the baptized have lost a living sense of the faith, or even no longer consider themselves members of the Church, and live a life far removed from Christ and his Gospel. In this case, what is needed is a "new evangelization" or a "re-evangelization" (*The Mission*, 33).[8]

What else need be said?

Unfortunately, however, this still does not settle the issue for some Catholics. From laity and clergy alike, I hear a common question in response to this type of teaching, a question which would be well worth addressing now.

THEN WHAT ABOUT THE SACRAMENTS?

Many Catholics are under the impression that the mere act of receiving the sacraments is the prime mover in salvation. I've even heard such concepts come out of the mouths of bishops. These Catholics have not been introduced to (or sometimes even ignore) a solid understanding of sacraments, how they work, and how they relate to salvation. Twenty-five years before John Paul II wrote the previously quoted statement, the Second Vatican Council admitted to the fact that, in the Catholic Church, there are "those who seem to understand or believe little of what they practice" (*Life of Priests*, 4).[9] So, *what about the sacraments?*

A governing principle was distinctly and clearly articulated in the Council's document dealing with worship and the sacraments:

> The sacred liturgy does not exhaust the entire activity of the Church. Before men can come

> to the liturgy they must be called to faith and
> conversion...[10]

Note, "before" we discuss worship and sacraments (liturgy). The sacramental life of Christianity is designed for those who have already faced the conversion issue and possess the faith content therein. The principle is this: liturgical acts are not the be-all and end-all of the Church; faith content spiritually precedes the inclination to sacramentalize.

And, of course, this governing principle simply echoes a long-standing tradition of biblical revelation—external rituals, in and of themselves, carry little weight with God. As far back as the Old Testament, the prophets railed against people whose rituals did not express a heart in alignment with what the rite was meant to symbolize and do.[*] It would be like two people getting married, even though they weren't in love. In the New Testament, John the Baptist, greatest of old covenant prophets (cf. Matt. 11:11), ministered a sacramental ritual. Yet he chased away those who came lacking the inner repentance his sacrament expressed, urging them to "go there" first and then come to the ritual (cf. Matthew 3:7–9.) The Savior Himself spoke more about *how* to do rituals in a spiritually appropriate way (fasting, worship, offering, sacrifice), than He did about the importance of the rituals themselves. And the theological tradition of the Catholic Church has extended the same accentuation down to the present. Notice the emphasis:

> What faith confesses, the sacraments communi-
> cate... (*Catechism*, 1692).[11]

---

[*] Fr. Bob Bedard, the founder of a new community of priests who are very much concerned over this issue, actually called this an abuse of the sacraments. (Bob Bedard, "Abusing the Sacraments", in *Companions of the Cross Newsletter*, Summer 2001: 1–2.)

If there is no *faith* content (inner adherence to what the act is all about), the sacraments have nothing to "communicate." They are empty copies of otherwise authentic actions. The sacraments "presuppose faith" (*Sacred Liturgy*, 59).[12]

Unfortunately, what many Catholics were taught *de facto* about sacraments amounts to little more than magic. The thinking goes, "If the ritual is done properly, grace is given supernaturally; and that's all that's needed." But official Catholic teaching has always emphasized that sacrementality is a two-way street. (Everything we said in chapter seven on the need to *receive* the gift of salvation, is but an example of this reality.) A general principle of the spiritual life is that, if one has the capacity of reason, he or she must cooperate with God's grace to release its intended results. In the fourth century, St. Basil said "For nothing that is not deliberate is to be pronounced blessed."[13] So, while affirming that God can be relied on to do what He promises to do through a sacrament:

> Nevertheless, the fruits of the sacraments also depend on the disposition of the one who receives them (*Catechism*, 1128).[14]

> Catholic theology recognizes the concept of a valid but bound sacrament. A sacrament is called bound if the fruit that should accompany it remains bound because of certain blocks that prevent its effectiveness... (Cantalamessa, *Baptism in the Holy Spirit*).[15]

So, how does a person properly *dispose* him or herself in a sacrament? How can we avail ourselves to its proper faith content, and not block out God's intention for the sacrament?

> For these are sacraments of faith and faith is
> born of the Word... (*Life of Priests*, 4).[16]

A Catholic must first be in touch with what the Word of God has to say about the particular aspect of Christianity being sacramentalized: a sacrament is nothing less than an acted out response to the Word. What the Word says precedes in importance what the sacraments express. Note the shocking preaching of the fifteenth century Franciscan St. Bernardine of Siena:

> And if between these two things—either to hear
> Mass or hear a sermon—you can only do one,
> you must miss Mass rather than the sermon;
> the reason for this is that there is less danger to
> your soul in not hearing Mass than there is in
> not hearing the sermon...[17]

Sacraments can do what they're intended to do only if the person responds in faith to what the Word is calling for in that particular sacramental moment.

So strong is the necessity of this *disposition* that, without it (the Catholic Church teaches) one could come to a sacrament and actually "receive it in vain" (*Sacred Liturgy*, 11).[18] Now, to do anything *in vain* means that the intended effect of the action was never achieved, time and energy has been wasted, and it would have been better never to have done the action at all. This is what the Catholic Church teaches about its sacraments. And the impact on the lived life of a Catholic can be summarized by something Cardinal Edward Cassidy said in an address while he was President of the Pontifical Council for Promoting Christian Unity:

It is, after all, much more important that a person find salvation in Christ than that he or she belong without conviction to any particular community. [19]

BAPTISM AND THE GOSPEL

We see these principles most clearly applied in my Church's teaching on the relationship between baptism, the gospel, and salvation. Three points are noteworthy.

1. The Catholic Church teaches that we do not substitute baptism for the gospel.

> ...The Church evangelizes when she seeks to convert, solely through the divine power of the Message she proclaims... (*On Evangelization*, 18).[20]

Notice, this says nothing about imparting Christianity through the use of the sacraments or through any external practice of Catholic religion. Though these have their appropriate place, evangelizing happens *solely* (did you hear that?) through the divine power of the "message" we preach—the *kerygma*. The Second Vatican Council's description of our Church's missionary mandate carefully spelled out this dynamic.

> Thus, reborn by the Word of God (cf. 1 Pet. 1:23), men may through baptism be joined to that Church which, as the Body of the Word Incarnate, is nourished and lives by the Word of God and by the Eucharistic Bread (cf. Acts 2:43). (*Missionary Activity*, 6).[21]

Rebirth comes by the *Word*, leading to connection with the Body of Christ in baptism, and only then, to the rest of revelation and the sacraments.

2. Like all sacraments, baptism must be entered into with the proper disposition for it to do what it was intended to do.

> By the sacrament of baptism, whenever it is properly conferred in the way the Lord determined, and received with the appropriate dispositions of soul, a man becomes truly incorporated into the crucified and glorified Christ and is reborn to a sharing of the divine life... (*Ecumenism*, 22).[22]

> They [the followers of Christ] are justified in the Lord Jesus, and through baptism sought in faith they truly become sons of God and sharers in the divine nature (*On the Church*, 40).[23]

Baptism is not an unqualified ritual. Its goal is achieved only if "received with the appropriate dispositions," and sought in *faith* which (as we've already seen) only arises as a response to the word of salvation. This is the context in which we must understand anything Catholicism teaches about baptism. This sacrament never stands alone—it is "linked at the hip" to faith in the gospel. [24] John Paul II tied together this, and the previous point, in a succinct way:

> ...the initial proclamation has a central and irreplaceable role, since it introduces man into the mystery of the love of God, who invites

him to enter a personal relationship with him in Christ and opens the way to conversion. Faith is born of preaching, and every ecclesial community draws its origin and life from the personal response of each believer to that preaching (*The Redeemer*, 44).[25]

3. Baptism is not a *work* we have to do in order to merit or earn our salvation.

Whatever in the justified precedes or follows the free gift of faith is neither the basis of justification nor merits it (*Joint Declaration*, 25).[26]

THEN WHAT ABOUT...

Infant baptism? This is, of course, an issue over which there has been considerable debate right from the early centuries of the Church. And it is also an issue about which even present-day Evangelicals are not in complete agreement. To weigh in on the position supporting infant baptism would take us beyond the scope of this book. What is germane to our purpose, however, is to demonstrate this affirmation of the Catholic Church: people baptized before being capable of conversion still need to respond to the gospel when they become able. We have already seen in Paul VI's *On Evangelization in the Modern World* that the first proclamation is addressed especially to those who have not heard it "or to children."[27] Baptized children are grouped with those who have not heard the message and who need to. The *Catechism of the Catholic Church* expands on this concept:

> By its very nature infant Baptism requires a
> *post-baptismal catechumenate.* [28]

Please bear with the vocabulary here, because this statement
has profound implications.

- Infant baptism has a unique *nature*: in other
  words, we wouldn't expect it to perform in exactly
  the same way as adult baptism does.

- Its nature requires a *catechumenate after* it. The
  catechumenate is the process by which a person
  investigates Christianity in the Catholic Church—
  a process that is to be preceded by evangelization.*
  In the case of infants, therefore, what normally
  precedes baptism must nevertheless occur after it:
  hearing, understanding, and personally responding to the gospel.

- This is *required* by the very nature of infant baptism. Implied, but not stated is that since this
  person is not capable of hearing, understanding,
  and responding to the salvation message at the
  time of baptism, when the time comes that he or
  she *is* able, he or she *must* do so. Sacramentaliza-
  tion is no substitute for evangelization.

Likewise, the very Instruction on Baptism for Children in
the Roman Rite states:

---

* Thus, in Rite of Christian Initiation for Adults, Introduction, we read: "It [the period preceding
the catechumenate] is a time of evangelization: faithfully and constantly the living God is proclaimed
and Jesus Christ whom he has sent for the salvation of all. Thus those who are not yet Christians, their
hearts opened by the Holy Spirit, may believe and be fully converted to the Lord and commit themselves sincerely to him."[29].

Christian formation [of baptized children], which is their due, seeks to lead them gradually to learn God's plan in Christ, so that they may ultimately accept for themselves the faith in which they have been baptized.[30]

Simply put, "The infant baptized, must be evangelized."

Another key text is one to which we keep returning on this issue, the *Catechism of the Catholic Church* (cf. 1427). It also states that baptism is the "principal place for the first and fundamental conversion."[31] That implies it's not the *only* place. Infant baptism provides a prime example. In this case, the other dynamic (the first and fundamental conversion) comes later. What is clear however (as we have already seen), is that it *must* occur on the part of one who is capable of "faith in the gospel": it then becomes a necessary response of one who "renounces evil and gains salvation, that is, the forgiveness of all sins and the gift of new life."[32]

The Church's teaching covers all grounds and basically calls out to its members: If for any reason you didn't *get* the message at the time of baptism,* you cannot ignore it when it comes your way by hiding behind the sacrament. No baptized person who can hear, understand, and respond to the *kerygma* is exempt from doing so if he or she still wishes to be saved.

As surprising at this may sound to both Catholics and non-Catholics alike, Church history evidences the fact that the issue is nothing new. As far back as the turn of the third century, the Church father Tertullian criticized the tendency to ascribe salvation to the ritual of baptism alone:

---

* This also addresses cases which exist in Evangelical circles as well as in the Catholic Church: adults who are baptized without having been converted.

> A presumptuous confidence in baptism
> introduces all kinds of vicious delay and tergi-
> versation [unprincipled fickleness] with regard
> to repentance.[33]

> How inconsistent is it to expect pardon of sins
> to be granted to a repentance which they have
> not fulfilled![34]

In *On Baptism, Against the Donatists*, St. Augustine emphasized that the inner realities preside over the outer realities of
baptism:

> Or how are they saved by water, who, making
> a bad use of holy baptism, though they seem
> to be within [the Church], yet persevere to the
> end of their days in a wicked and abandoned
> course of life? [35]

Notice: there is such a thing as "bad use" of baptism in the
first place. It's as we've been saying all along: a sacrament—which
means baptism as well—never stands alone. Here Augustine
clarifies that the inner realities of baptism take precedence. We
err if we use the sacrament of primary conversion but have not
a converted heart, or use the sacrament of initiation and participate in a converted community, but do not intend to live
the converted lifestyle. And, lest we underestimate the seriousness of this discrepancy, Augustine moves the exhortation a
step further by an illustration with the biblical prefigurement
of baptism—Noah's ark:

> As, therefore, it was not another but the
> same water that saved those who were placed

within the ark, and destroyed those who were left without the ark, so it is not by different baptisms, but by the same, that good Catholics are saved, and bad Catholics, or heretics, perish.[36]

Don't bypass this. What he's saying is not only that the baptism of one who ignores primary conversion is meaningless, he is taking what we've already affirmed about the sacraments, to the *nth* degree. When it comes to baptism, one who dismisses the accompanying first and fundamental conversion has not only received that sacrament in vain but has thereby made the biggest mistake of his or her eternity. For in such a case, on the Day of Judgment the moment of baptism will actually stand as a testimony *against* the person, *and* become the very *cause*, not of salvation, but of its exact opposite—*eternal separation from God.*

Our conclusion is that whatever one thinks about infant baptism, the Catholic Church teaches, and has taught in the past, that the baptism of infants is anything but a "get-out-of-evangelization-free" card. I can think of no better way to summarize the issue than by this quote from Fr. Raniero Cantalamessa, preacher to the papal household:

> In the case of baptism, what is it that causes the fruit of the sacrament to stay bound? The sacraments are not magical rituals that act mechanically, without the person's knowledge, disregarding any response on his part. Their effectiveness is the fruit of a synergy or cooperation between divine omnipotence— in reality the grace of Christ or the Holy

Spirit—and human freedom. As St. Augustine said, "the one who created you without your cooperation will not save you without your cooperation."[37]

The Word of salvation, then baptism, and then the rest of the Christian dispensation—in that order of importance. Indeed, at least in the Catholic Church, it's time for a "re-evangelization."

10

THE FISHBOWL REVISITED

Indeed, in nothing is the power of the Dark Lord
more clearly shown than in the estrangement
that divides all those who still oppose him.[1]

—HALDIR, THE ELF

SOLA GRATIA, SOLA *fide, solo Christo*—by grace alone,
through faith alone, because of Christ alone. These were
the bywords of the Protestant Reformation. And they were
words which divided Christianity… bitterly. But with the process of charitable dialogue and labor, they are now words which
unite. Having listened to and clarified the precise meanings of
the terms raised by the Protestant Reformation, the Catholic
Church now teaches, along with the followers of Luther:

> Justification takes place "by grace alone"; by
> faith alone the person is justified "apart from
> works" (Rom. 3:28). (Annex to the Official
> Common Statement on the *Joint Declaration
> on the Doctrine of Justification*, Annex 2C).[2]

> Through Christ alone are we justified, when we receive this salvation in faith (*Joint Declaration*, 16).[3]

> ...thus it becomes clear that the mutual condemnations of former times do not apply to the Catholic and Lutheran doctrines of justification as they are presented in the Joint Declaration (*Joint Declaration*, Annex 1).[4]

That barrier is removed. It's up to us to see it so.

And thus, we need new vision. Actually, for Catholics, it's an old vision. It was articulated in 1964 at the Second Vatican Council in its *Decree on Ecumenism*:

> Nor should we forget that whatever is wrought by the grace of the Holy Spirit in the hearts of our separated brethren can contribute to our own edification. Whatever is truly Christian never conflicts with the genuine interests of the faith; indeed it can always result in a more ample realization of the very mystery of Christ and the Church.[5]

> ...Catholics must joyfully acknowledge and esteem the truly Christian endowments from our common heritage which are to be found among our separated brethren. It is right and salutary to recognize the riches of Christ and virtuous works in the lives of others who are bearing witness to Christ...[6]

And that vision spawned greater clarity for Catholics about the very events of the Reformation, and about Martin Luther, himself:

> Who...would still deny that Martin Luther was a deeply religious person who with honesty and dedication sought for the message of the gospel? Who would deny that in spite of the fact that he fought against the Roman Catholic Church and the Apostolic See—and for the sake of truth one must not remain silent about this*—he retained a considerable part of the old Catholic faith? Indeed, is it not true that the Second Vatican Council has even implemented requests that were first expressed by Martin Luther, among others, and as a result of which many aspects of Christian faith and life now find better expression than they did before? To be able to say this in spite of all the differences is a reason for great joy and much hope (Cardinal Johannes Willebrands, address at the Lutheran World Federation's Fifth Assembly).[8]

> Luther has in an extraordinary way made a new starting point for theology and Christian

---

* In the period immediately following Luther's stand at the Diet of Worms, hope for reconciliation was not completely abandoned. Pope Adrian—who himself had no particular liking for Luther—nevertheless sent the following instructions with his representative to the Diet of Nurnberg: You are also to say that we frankly acknowledge that...for many years things deserving of abhorrence have gathered around the Holy See. Sacred things have been misused, ordinances transgressed, so that in everything there has been a change for the worse. Thus it is not surprising that the malady has crept down from the head to the members, from popes to the hierarchy. We all, prelates and clergy, have gone astray from the right way....Therefore in our name give promises that we shall use all diligence to reform before all things the Roman Curia.[7] (Also, in 2000, section 1.1 of a work John Paul II requested of the International Theological Commission, *Memory and Reconciliation: The Church and the Faults of the Past*, translates the above using terms such as "abominations", "abuses", "lies" and "deep-rooted and extensive...sickness".)

life for the times coming (Cardinal Johannes Willebrands, address at the Lutheran World Federation's Fifth Assembly).[9]

It is possible for us today to learn from Luther together...

- As a theologian, preacher, pastor, hymn-writer and man of prayer, Luther has extraordinary spiritual force witnessed anew to the biblical message of God's gift of liberating righteousness and made it shine forth.

- Luther directs us to the priority of God's work in the life, teaching and service of the Church.

- He calls us to a faith which is absolute trust in the God who in the life, death and resurrection of his Son has shown himself to be gracious to us.

- He teaches us to understand grace as a personal relationship of God to human beings which is unconditional and frees from fear of God's wrath and for service of one another.

- He testifies that God's forgiveness is the only basis and hope for human life.

- He calls the Church to constant renewal by the Word of God.

- He teaches us that unity in essentials allows for differences in custom, order and theology.

- He reminds theologians that knowledge of God's mercy reveals itself only in

prayer and meditation. It is the Holy
Spirit who persuades us of the truth in
the gospel and keeps and strengthens us
in that truth in spite of all temptations
("Martin Luther: Witness to Jesus
Christ").[10]

In fact, the scientific researches of the Evangelical and Catholic scholars, researches whose
results have already reached notable points
of convergence, have led to the delineation
of a more complete and more differentiated
picture of Luther's personality and of the
complex historical realities of the first half of
the sixteenth century. Consequently there is
clearly outlined the deep religious feeling of
Luther, who was driven with burning passion
by the question of eternal salvation (John Paul
II, letter to Cardinal Willebrands).[11]

Today it is more important than ever that all
Christians bring their particular gifts and
charisms to the spiritual life of Europe, so that
each one can learn from the richness of the
other. Protestant Christianity has enriched all
Christianity with its religious songs, its great
Church music, and its constant theological
(John Paul II speech, Germany, 1996).[12]

Now in these statements no leader is pretending that there
aren't many other issues needing to be addressed, or that we
are already unified as the Master prayed we would be in John
17. Some breeds of fish, when put into the fishbowl with other

breeds, still tend to fight. And on that score we continue to need nothing less than grace from above in our goal of full unity.

> ...this Synod declares its realization that the holy task of reconciling all Christians in the unity of the one and only Church of Christ transcends human energies and abilities. It therefore places its hope entirely in the prayer of Christ for the Church, in the love of the Father for us, and in the power of the Holy Spirit. "And hope does not disappoint, because the charity of God is poured forth in our hearts by the Holy Spirit who has been given to us" (Rom. 5:5). (*Ecumenism*, 24).[13]

As we mentioned in the very first chapter, the Spirit can be relied upon to supply what we need in order to follow the unity instincts He Himself has placed in our hearts. With this vision, and with this indispensable grace, our task is to "go forward without obstructing the ways of divine Providence and without prejudicing the future inspiration of the Holy Spirit" (*Ecumenism*, 24).[14] *

---

* In 1985, for example, Cardinal Johannes Willebrands (then head of the Vatican Secretariat for Christian Unity) was heard to say at the Extraordinary Synod in Rome, "*Return* is not a word in our ecumenical vocabulary."[15] I agree with Fr. Richard John Neuhaus' following assessment of this statement, and I believe it to be a worthy commentary on this phrase from the *Decree on Ecumenism* (24) you just read: The continuing conversion to which we are all called does entail turnings and returnings of many kinds, but the invitation that Rome issues to Evangelicals and others today cannot be described simply in terms of "Return to Mother Church.'" Rather, Rome asks, "What can we do, and what can you do, and what can we do together to overcome the divisions that are manifestly contrary to the will of God for the Christian people?" The Catholic Church does not claim to have all the answers to those questions. Only God knows what will be the result of this encounter between Evangelicals and Catholics. Certainly, both Evangelicals and Catholics will be changed by it. The invitation and the questions do not come with an organizational blueprint or a schedule of ecumenical actions.[16]

The Next Steps

So, in the end, I am with you and you are with me in this reality called Christianity. We cannot change the fact that God has put us in the same fish bowl. If we choose to build together on the foundation of our same gospel, two things will determine the success of our next steps.

First, repentance.

> There can be no ecumenism worthy of the name without a change of heart (*Ecumenism,* 7).[17]

Thus, I want to end this book by coming into personal agreement with what the Second Vatican Council Fathers wrote:

> Thus, in humble prayer, we beg pardon of God and of our separated brethren, just as we forgive those who trespass against us (*Ecumenism,* 7).[18]

I will not judge the hearts of the men who first expressed this sentiment: God has reserved that privilege to Himself. Rest assured, if there was a shred of insincerity or inauthenticity in these men, He *will* judge them! But let me restate that, for my part, I grieve over the sinful bitterness that has been held in the hearts of Catholics toward Evangelicals and toward Martin Luther himself, and I lament any ungodly treatment that stemmed from it. If we are what we claim to be, we owe the first apology to you; our teachings even state that we are on for "making the first approaches toward" you (*Ecumenism,* 7).[19]

So, right now,
    As an ordained leader in the Catholic Church,
    I identify with these sins of bitterness
    On the part of Catholics, both past and present.
    And I repent to you,
    My Evangelical brothers and sisters,
    And ask—
    No, I beg
    Your forgiveness,
    So that God,
    As He always does,
    Will raise up something marvelous
    From the dust and ashes of this sin.

I thank You, Father,
    For every Evangelical Christian
    Who has just accepted this repentance
    And extended forgiveness.
    This is truly a miracle of Your grace, Father,
    As will be what our own eyes see You do in response.

I have been encouraged by the Evangelical brethren who have already exhibited this spirit of reconciliation. A while back, I had a conversation with one of the vice presidents of Promise Keepers. It was the first time I had ever heard someone say, "We Evangelicals need to stop fighting the battles of the sixteenth century." In a similar vein, Chuck Colson, another notable Evangelical leader, wrote:

> Interdenominational strife is not as prevalent
> as it once was, but it still occurs—and often in
> a way that mars the witness of the Body. A few
> years ago an international group of Evangelical

leaders met to prepare for a large conference in a country which happened to be predominantly Catholic. Since the conference was on a universal subject—evangelism—I urged that Catholic Evangelicals be invited. "Never," one of the participants shouted, slamming his fist on the table. "We fought that battle four hundred years ago, and we're not going to surrender now." Apparently he wanted to continue the Reformation warfare. A cease-fire would spoil his fun.

He prevailed, and as a result the political leaders in the country snubbed the conference; the local Catholic bishop, himself an Evangelical in the renewal movement, on the closing day of the conference, led a separate evangelistic rally. All of this, of course, was widely reported by the press.

In view of all this, it is not difficult to understand the two most frequent responses people give for avoiding church: "All Christians are hypocrites," and "Christians are always fighting with each other."

To the first, I invariably reply, "Sure, probably so. Come on and join us. You'll feel right at home." But I haven't come up with a good answer to the second.

Holding the Church to its historic faith, both in its practices and institutions, is a necessary corrective. But shouldn't it be done in love and with understanding, showing grace instead of rancor?[20]

Powerful point! He goes on to share his insight into this matter:

> Rancor not only destroys witness, it also exposes weakness of conviction. The less secure people are in their beliefs, the more strident they become. Conversely, the more confident people are of the truth, the more grace they exhibit in those who don't agree.[21]

And this leads to the other determinant in our next steps together: each *breed* of Christians in the born-again fishbowl can no longer to ignore the challenge the others bring. Rather, we must actually embrace it as the growth pains of the Body of Christ.

So to my Evangelical brethren I say, "Here come the document-based Catholics!" I have made it a life project to educate Catholics out of the spiritual sloth of leaning on rumors or falsehoods they've been told about what our Church teaches. And I insist that Catholics who do study our official documents, integrate what they read into the "full counsel of teaching," rather than use it as isolated proof text. Yes, there is a new *breed* of document-based *Evangelical Catholics* arising, the likes of which you have not encountered before. We have something to contribute to the Body, and we are not going away.

And to my fellow Catholics, I say this: our teaching no longer allows us to play the "Counter Reformation trump card" when confronted by Evangelicals. In other words, we can no longer hide behind the defensive superiority or triumphalism that once characterized many sectors of our Church in the face of Protestantism. That posture was buried at the Second Vatican Council and is no longer in service. Reread the visionary quotes from paragraph four of Vatican II's *Decree on Ecumenism* cited earlier in this chapter. What these texts basically tell us is that whatever is truly Christian that is found among non-Catholics *will build us up* as Catholics.

> All these blessings come from Christ and lead to him, (cf. *Decree on Ecumenism*, 3), and are in themselves calls to "Catholic unity" (cf. *Dogmatic Constitution on the Church* 8). (*Catechism*, 819)[22]

Particularly when Evangelicals want to do one of the things they do best—evangelize us—these texts show that we can accept the Christian salvation message from non-Catholics without leaving the Catholic Church. Yes, we have a right to disagree on issues other than the gospel, issues about which we, in fact, differ. And we can and should respond to any claims about Catholicism arising from ignorance of our official teachings. This book has equipped you to begin to do so.

But, the bottom line is this: Catholics who simply avoid the gospel by playing that Counter-Reformation trump card, those who respond to Protestant evangelizers with the reflex, "Oh no, here come the Evangelicals," will also, in the same breath, have to respond, "Oh no, here comes the Pope, his Church's teachings, and document-based Catholicism," because all these profess the *same* gospel!

The challenge is, indeed, great. But I, for one, am excited by the new wineskins God has provided for us to usher in the Kingdom in a fresh way.

I close with a story. The evangelist in our ministry whom I mentioned in chapter nine, Arlene, takes a cab occasionally. When appropriate, she uses that opportunity to share the gospel also. Often enough she rides with a Muslim driver. If so, in her very non-threatening style, she begins dialoguing about the apparent commonalities between Islam and Christianity. Eventually they get around to the obvious difference when it comes to salvation. She often initiates this by asking the Muslim what his plans are after leaving planet earth. Humble Muslims who know their Quran will relate their dread of final judgment. This opens the door to talk about the difference Jesus can make in one's eternity. In one such conversation, a driver was rapt in attention to what Arlene was sharing. It seemed to her that, as in so many other cases, this Muslim had never heard the truths of the gospel explained to him before. When she finished speaking of God's plan of salvation through Jesus' atonement on the cross and the gift of grace now available to us, with no prompting whatsoever, this Muslim spontaneously responded, *That's good news!*

It *is* good news. It's *very* good news. And it's the joy of our lives to bear this message containing an eternal impact on those who first hear and receive it. But the gospel continues to be good news in yet another way for us born-again Christians who *have* accepted it, if we dare to believe that, in spite of our differences and even disagreements, the one and the same salvation message is the foundation on which we all stand and upon which we all wish to build.

History has shown us that the Iron Curtain, once thought impenetrable, could indeed come down given the right influences. I believe the Holy Spirit is speaking the same to us about our own "Stained Glass Curtain." When both sides of this divide are "stained," not as masterpieces of our own human religious doing, but with the blood of Jesus—with the influence of accepting the true salvation of His gospel—our "curtain" can begin to come down as well. Let's dare to start "crossing" the Evangelical–Catholic divide, acknowledging that the cross and its message are indeed "our common heritage."

Epilogue

THE INVITATION

PERHAPS READING CHAPTERS four through seven was the first time you've heard of the plan of salvation spelled out so specifically. And perhaps, though some of it was not unfamiliar, you heard other things you never heard before. If you're a Catholic, maybe you simply had no idea what our Church really teaches on this subject. And, whether Catholic, Protestant, non-denominational, inter-denominational, or someone who doesn't even consider himself a Christian, maybe you have now come to the all-important understanding of your own sin problem and its consequences.

If you are under conviction by the Holy Spirit about sin and have been "cut to the heart" by the message (Acts 2:37); if you can honestly say that you are hopeless, helpless, desperate and lost because of sin; and you know that you are in need of nothing less than a divine Savior; then this chapter is for you. I simply could not lay out the most important truths about our lives, without then offering a reader like you the opportunity to accept and be transformed by the good news.

If you have never before personally received God's gift of salvation and are ready to do so now, first take a moment to get in touch with the pain of your rebellion and independence before God. Enter into the grief and offense that it causes your heavenly Father and embrace the *dread* of that helplessness, as

Paul the Apostle did when he said, "What a wretched man I am! Who will rescue me from this body doomed to death?" (Rom. 7:24).

Now pour out your heart to God in a once and for all repentance and conversion of life. Make a choice to turn away from this rebellious and independent nature. Tell Him that you believe what Jesus did to save you and transform you. Give up trying to change yourself. Transfer your sin and its consequences to the Lamb of God who takes away the sin of the world (cf. John 1:29). Surrender to Him as your Lord—owner and controller. And then, in faith, accept His gift of rebirth to a new life.

If you're having a hard time expressing what's inside, these words can help you. There's nothing magical or automatic about them; they will do nothing if they don't really voice your heart's desire. But if they can help you to do just that, come to the Lord right now and pray:

Father,
I come to You just as I am—
A weak, needy sinner.
I confess that my desire to live my own life
Without dependence on You
Has produced things that displease You.
But, I am tired of being controlled by self,
And I acknowledge
That it's this rebellion and independence
That really offends You.
So I'm coming back home as a prodigal child.
I want to do it Your way.
I repent once and for all
Of a life lived under the mastery of sin.

But, though I'm powerless,
  I believe You can save me.
  I believe that what Jesus did on the cross
  Was enough to break the hold of sin on my life
  And make of me a new creature pleasing to You.
  So I invite You to be my Savior.
  I put my trust now only in His shed blood
  To forgive me and make me right with You.

And now, in this new life, Jesus,
  I invite You to take over my heart.
  I surrender my will to You
  And ask You to live Your life in me
  By the Holy Spirit.
  I gladly receive Your salvation
  And enter into the new and everlasting
  Covenant.

Thank You,
  Father, Son, and Holy Spirit,
  That I am now a new creation.
  Thank You that I have the precious gift of
  Salvation.
  By Your power alone,
  I look forward to loving You and serving You
  The rest of my days,
  Until, by Your grace
  I meet You face to face.
  Amen!
  Amen!
  Amen!

(Right here, take some time to rejoice with the whole company of heaven... They're sure rejoicing with you! [cf. Luke 15:7].)

If you have sincerely received salvation, I welcome you into the family of God. If you haven't already gotten baptized, make arrangements to do so at once (cf. Mark 16:16). All Christians agree that it is the Lord's will to express salvation in this prophetic gesture.

In order to find support in living the new life, find a community of people who have received this salvation also. How do you know? They are individuals who have their own stories about how this happened, just as you now do, and they'll tell you about it. Find them, and join in meeting with them. We are meant to be a Body, and we need one another by God's design.

Also, feed your new life each day by praying and reading and studying the Word of God. You will also grow the more you learn to witness Jesus and His message of salvation to the world around you. God will build your new life around these four pillars—prayer, Scripture, fellowship, and witness.

My sincere hope is that you will indeed continue to grow and grow, my brother or sister. It is a blessing to me to have witnessed the truth of God's eternal Word, and my intention is to meet you on the last day, if not before.

Until that day comes, join your newfound family in this prayer, first penned by the apostle Paul, unifying born-again believers in every era and especially in such a time as this:

> Glory be to him whose power, working in us, can do infinitely more than we can ask or imagine; glory be to him from generation to generation in the Church and in Christ Jesus forever and ever. Amen.
>
> —EPHESIANS 3:20–21

Notes

Chapter 1

1. Richard Neuhaus and Charles Colson, eds., "The Catholic Difference," in *Evangelicals and Catholics Together: Toward a Common Mission* (Nashville, TN: Thomas Nelson, Inc. 1995), 199–200.

2. Abraham Kuyper, *Lectures on Calvinism* (1931; repr., Grand Rapids, MI: William B. Eerdmans Pub. Co., 2000), 184.

3. Web site: www.scienceray.com (accessed April 21, 2010).

4. Paul D. Molnar, "The Theology of Justification in Dogmatic Context" in eds. Mark Husbands and Daniel J. Treier, *Justification: What's at Stake in the Current Debates* (Downers Grove, IL: InterVarsity Press, 2004), 229.

5. Geoffrey Wainwright, "The Ecclesial Scope of Justification," Husbands and Treier, *Justification*, 273.

6. Vatican II, *Decree on Ecumenism*, 4.

7. Ibid., *Decree on the Ministry and Life of Priests*, 4.

8. Web site: www.greatcom.org/english/four.htm (accessed April 21, 2010).

9. Promise Keepers event, Mar. 8, 1996.

10. *Ecumenism*, 1.

11. John Paul II, *Toward the Third Millennium*, apostolic letter, November 10, 1994, 34–35, from Web site: www.vatican. va/holy_father/john_paul_ii/apost_letters/documents/hf_jp-ii_apl_10111994_tertio-millennio-adveniente_en.html (accessed April 21, 2010).

12. John Paul II, *That They May Be One*, 3, 11, from Web site: www. vatican.va/holy_father/john_paul_ii/encyclicals/documents/hf_ jp-ii_enc_25051995_ut-unum-sint_en.htm.

13. Ibid., 88; Vatican II, *Ecumenism*, 7.

14. John Paul II, *That They May Be One*, 63.

15. *Joint Declaration on the Doctrine of Justification*, 40 from Web site: www.vatican.va/roman_curia/pontifical_councils/chrstuni/documents/rc_pc_chrstuni_doc_31101999_cath-luth-joint-declaration_en.html (accessed April 21, 2010).

CHAPTER 2

1. Raleigh Washington and Glen Kehren, *Breaking Down the Walls* (Chicago: Moody Press, 1997), 23.

2. Vatican II, *Life of Priests*, 16.

3. Washington and Kehren, *Breaking*, 109.

4. *Joint Declaration*, 40.

5. John Paul II, *That They May Be One*, 63.

6. Vatican II, *Ecumenism*, 6.

CHAPTER 3

1. Web site: www.wayfaring.info/2006/11/30/the-leaning-tower-of-pisa-is-the-worlds-most-famous-construction-mistake (accessed April 21, 2010).

2. Paul VI, *On Evangelization in the Modern World*, apostolic exhortation, December 8, 1975, 52, from Web site: www.vatican.va/holy_father/paul_vi/apost_exhortations/documents/hf_p-vi_exh_19751208_evangelii-nuntiandi_en.html (accessed April 20, 2010).

3. Vatican II, *Ecumenism*, 11.

4. Paul VI, *On Evangelization*, 25.

5. Vatican II, *Ecumenism*, 6.

6. Ibid., *Decree on the Missionary Activity of the Church*, 6.

7. Raniero Cantalamessa, "Faith in Christ Today and at the Beginning of the Church," 2, *Homilies in the Papal Household*, December 2, 1995, from Web site: www.cantalamessa.org/en/predicheView.php?id=69 (accessed April 20, 2010).

8. Paul VI, *On Evangelization*, 52.

9. *Catechism of the Catholic Church*, 6, from Web site: www.vatican.va/archive/ENG0015/_INDEX.HTM (accessed April 20, 2010).

10. *On Evangelization*, 25.

11. Cantalamessa, "Faith in Christ Today," 3.

CHAPTER 4

1. Oliver Wendell Holmes, Jr., "Law and the Court" (speech, Harvard Law School Association of New York, February 15, 1913).

2. *Catechism*, 1.

3. Ibid., 27.

4. Vatican II, *Missionary Activity*, 13; John Paul II, *The Mission of the Redeemer*, 44, from Web site: www.vatican.va/holy_father/john_paul_ii/encyclicals/documents/hf_jp-ii_enc_07121990_redemptoris-missio_en.html (accessed April 20, 2010).

5. *Catechism*, 2558.

6. St. Isaac the Syrian, *Ascetical Homilies 28*, from Web site: www.ldysinger.stjohnsem.edu/@texts/0700_isaac-nin/00a_start_htm (accessed April 20, 2010).

7. St. Thomas Aquinas, *Summa Theologica* II-II, q. 11, art. 1: 13th century.

8. Gregory XVI, *Mirari Vos*, 22, from Web site: www.papalencyclicals.net/Greg16/g16mirar.htm (accessed April 20, 2010).

9. Benedict XVI, General Audience (St. Peter's Square, Rome, June 3, 2009).

10. John Paul II, *Crossing the Threshold of Hope* (New York: Alfred A. Knopf, Inc., 1994), 62–63.

11. Pseudo-Dionysius, *On the Divine Names*, 2.9, from Web site: www.ccel.org/ccel/pearse/morefathers/files/areopagite_03_divine_names.htm (accessed April 20, 2010).

12. St. Benedict of Aniane, *Munimenta Fidei*, in Dom Jean Leclercq, OSB, *Analecta Monastica* (Citta del Vaticano: Libreria Vaticana, 1948), 63.

13. St. Thomas Aquinas, *Summa Theologica* I, q. 13, art. 1.

14. John Paul II, *Catechesis in Our Time*, apostolic exhortation, 1979, 19, from Web site: www.vatican.va/holy_father/john_paul_ii/apost_exhortations/documents/hf_jp-ii_exh_16101979_catechesi-tradendae_en.html (accessed April 20, 2010).

15. Paul VI, *On Evangelization*, 26.

16. *Catechism*, 218.

17. Paul Josef Cordes, "The Call to the Catholic Charismatic Renewal from the Church Universal," trans. from *L'Osservatore Romano*, February 1–2, 1988.

18. Holmes, "Law and the Court."

CHAPTER 5

1. Vatican II, *Declaration on the Relationship of the Church to Non-Christian Religions*, 1.

2. Ibid., *Pastoral Constitution on the Church in the Modern World*, 13.

3. Ibid., 41.

4. Ibid., 58.

5. Ibid., 15.

6. Ibid., 18.

7. Ibid., *Decree on the Apostolate of the Laity*, 7.

8. *Catechism*, 1868.

9. "Introduction to the Rite of Penance," December 2, 1974, 5, from Web site: www.catholicliturgy.com/index.cfm/FuseAction/DocumentContents/Index/2/SubIndex/40/DocumentIndex/446 (accessed April 21, 2010).

10. *Catechism*, 1440.

11. Ibid., 2850.

12. Ibid., 408.

13. Ibid., 1869.

14. Vatican II, *Church in the Modern World*, 13.

15. *Catechism*, 387.

16. Ibid., 386.

17. Ibid., 1848.

18. John Paul II, *Crossing*, 57.

19. Vatican II, *Church in the Modern World*, 13.

20. *Catechism*, 1850.

21. Ibid., 1865.

22. Ibid.

23. *Joint Declaration on the Doctrine of Justification*, 19.

24.Vatican II, *Missionary Activity*, 3.

25.*Catechism*, 578.

26.Ibid., 400.

27.Vatican II, *Church in the Modern World*, 13.

28.Ibid., *Missionary Activity*, 8.

29.Ibid., *Church in the Modern World*, 45.

30.Paul VI, *On Evangelization*, 9.

31.*Catechism*, 588.

CHAPTER 6

1. Paul VI, *On Evangelization*, 27.

2. David Hume, *Dialogues Concerning Natural Religion*, (London: William Blackwood and Sons, 1907), 176. Washington quote from Web site: www.access.gpo.gove/congress/senate/farewell/sd106-21.pdf (accessed April 20, 2010).

3. *Catechism*, 571.

4. Paul VI, *On Evangelization*, 9.

5. *Catechism*, 615–616.

6. Paul VI, *On Evangelization*, 9.

7. *Catechism*, 571.

8. Ibid., 1991.

9. *Joint Declaration*, 15.

10.John Paul II, *Crossing*, 21.

11.*Basic Teachings for Catholic Religious Education*, National Conference of Catholic Bishops, January 11, 1973, 16.

12.*Catechism*, 654.

13.John Paul II, *The Redeemer of Humanity*, 18. www.vatican.va/holy_father/john_paul_ii/encyclicals/documents/hf_jp-ii_enc_04031979_redemptor-hominis_en.html (accessed April 21, 2010).

14.*Catechism*, 686.

15.Vatican II, *Church in the Modern World*, 22.

16.*Catechism*, 1997.

17.Ibid., 2003.

18.Paul VI, *On Evangelization*, 23.

19.John Paul II, *The Mission*, 5.

20.Vatican Congregation for the Doctrine of the Faith, *On the Unicity and Salvific Universality of Jesus Christ and the Church*, August 6, 2000, 15.

21.John Paul II, *The Redeemer*, 20.

22.*Catechism*, 616.

23.John Paul II, *Crossing*, 45.

24.John Paul II, *The Redeemer*, 36.

25.Paul VI, *On Evangelization*, 53.

26.Erwin Lutzer, *How Can You Be Sure That You Will Spend Eternity with God?* (Chicago: Moody Press, 1996), 13–14.

27.Vatican Congregation, *Salvific Universality*, 22.

28.Paul VI, *On Evangelization*, 53.

29.Vatican Congregation, *Salvific Universality*, 14.

30.Vatican II, *Missionary Activity*, 7.

Chapter 7

1. From Web site: http://supreme.justia.com/us/32/150/case.html (accessed April 20, 2010).

2. John Paul II, *Crossing*, 73–74.

3. Paul VI, *On Evangelization*, 27.

4. Vatican II, *Missionary Activity*, 7.

5. Vatican II, *Decree on the Ministry and Life of Priests*, 2.

6. Paul VI, *On Evangelization*, 23.

7. John Paul II, *Crossing*, 58.

8. John Paul II, *On the Holy Spirit in the Life of the Church and the World*, 31, from Web site: www.vatican.va/edocs/ENG0142/_INDEX.HTM (accessed April 20, 2010).

9. Joseph Conrad, *Lord Jim* (New York: Penguin Putnam Inc., 2000), 309.

10.*Joint Declaration*, 19.

11.*Catechism*, 1431.

12.Ibid., 1848.

13.Ibid., 368.

14.Ibid., 1431.

15.St. Augustine, "Sermon 352," *Works of Saint Augustine: A Translation for the 21st Century* (Hyde Park, NY: New City Press, 1995), 137.

16.John Paul II, *Crossing*, 73.

17.*Joint Declaration*, 16.

18.John Paul II, *The Mission*, 46.

19.Vatican II, *Dogmatic Constitution on Divine Revelation*, 5.

20.Cantalamessa, "Faith in Christ Today," 2.

21.Paul VI, *On Evangelization*, 10.

22.*Catechism*, 1226.

23.Vatican II, *Missionary Activity*, 13.

24.*Catechism*, 1427

25.Ibid.

CHAPTER 9

1. Billy Graham, "Do It Again, Lord!" in *Evangelizing Adults*, ed. Glenn C. Smith (Wheaton, IL: Tyndale House, 1985), 25.

2. Paul VI, *On Evangelization*, 52.

3. *The Texas Catholic* XIX, no. 10 (1970): 3.

4. John Paul II, *Catechesis*, 19.

5. The Barna Group, from Web site: www.barna.org, used with permission (accessed April 20, 2010).

6. Paul VI, *On Evangelization*, 25.

7. Ibid., 52.

8. John Paul II, *The Mission*, 33.

9. Vatican II, *Life of Priests*, 4.

10.Vatican II, *Constitution on the Sacred Liturgy*, 9.

11.*Catechism*, 1692.

12.Vatican II, *Sacred Liturgy*, 59.

13."Commentary on Psalm 33," 5 from *St. Basil: Exegetic Homilies*, translated by Sr. Agnes Clare Way, C.D.P. (Wachington D.C.: The Catholic University Press of America, 1963).

14.*Catechism*, 1128.

15.Cantalamessa, "Baptism in the Holy Spirit," teaching, from Web site: www.catholiccharismatic.us/ccc/articles/Cantalamessa/ Cantalamessa_002.html (accessed April 22, 2010).

16.Vatican II, *Life of Priests*, 4.

17.St. Bernardine, "Sermons of 1427 in Siena," in *The Preacher's Demons*, trans. Franco Mormando (Chicago: The University of Chicago Press, 1999), 3.

18.Vatican II, *Sacred Liturgy*, 11.

19.Cardinal Edward Cassidy (address at Meeting of North American Evangelicals and Catholics, October 1997), in *First Things* 79 (Jan. 1998): 24–26.

20.Paul VI, *On Evangelization*, 18.

21.Vatican II, *Missionary Activity*, 6.

22.Vatican II, *Ecumenism*, 22.

23.Vatican II, *On the Church*, 40.

24.Cf. *Catechism*, 1427.

25.John Paul II, *The Redeemer*, 44.

26.*Joint Declaration*, 25.

27.Paul VI, *On Evangelization*, 52.

28.*Catechism*, 1231.

29."Rite of Christian Initiation for Adults, Introduction," 9, from Web site: www.catholicliturgy.com/index.cfm/FuseAction/documentText/Index/14/SubIndex/0/ContentIndex/540/Start/539 (accessed April 20, 2010).

30."Rite of Baptism for Children," 3, from Web site: www.liturgyoffice.org.uk/Resources/Rites/Baptism-Children.pdf (accessed April 22, 2010).

31.*Catechism*, 1427.

32.Ibid.

33.Tertullian, "On Repentance," 6, from Web site: http://mb-soft.com/believe/txv/tertulls.htm (accessed April 22, 2010).

34.Ibid.

35.St. Augustine, *On Baptism, Against the Donatists*, 39, from Web site: http://mb-soft.com/believe/txue/august58.htm (accessed April 22, 2010).

36.Ibid.

37.Cantalamessa, "Baptism in the Holy Spirit."

Chapter 10

1. J. R. R. Tolkien, *The Fellowship of the Ring* (New York: Houghton Mifflin Co, 2005), 411.

2. *Joint Declaration*, Annex 2C.

3. *Joint Declaration*, 16.

4. *Joint Declaration*, Annex 1.

5. Vatican II, *Ecumenism*, 4.

6. Ibid.

7. Pope Adrian in *Pope, Council and World: The Story of Vatican II*, trans. Robert Blair Kaiser (New York: Macmillan Pub., 1963), 4.

8. Cardinal Johannes Willebrands, President of the Vatican Secretariat for Christian Unity (address at the Lutheran World Federation's Fifth Assembly, July 16, 1970).

9. Ibid.

10."Martin Luther: Witness to Jesus Christ" (Catholic-Lutheran Joint Commission, sponsored by the Pontifical Council for Promoting Christian Unity and the Lutheran World Federation, May 10, 1983).

11.John Paul II, letter to Cardinal Johannes Willebrands, President of the Vatican Secretariat for Christian Unity, October 31, 1983.

12.John Paul II (speech at Ecumenical Service in Paderborn, Germany, June 22, 1996).

13.Vatican II, *Ecumenism*, 24.

14.Ibid.

15.Neuhaus, *The Catholic Moment* (San Francisco: Harper and Row, 1987), 13.

16.Neuhaus and Colson, "The Catholic Difference," *Evangelical and Catholics Together*, 215.

17.Vatican II, *Ecumenism*, 7.

18.Ibid.

19.Ibid.

20.Charles Colson, *The Body* (Dallas, TX: Word Publishing, 1992), 101–102.

21.Ibid.

22.*Catechism*, 819.